OTHER TIMES,
OTHER PLACES

THE ARTHUR M. OKUN MEMORIAL LECTURES
Yale University

CHARLES L. SCHULTZE

OTHER TIMES, OTHER PLACES

Macroeconomic Lessons from U.S. and European History

With a Preface by James Tobin

THE BROOKINGS INSTITUTION
Washington, D.C.

Library of Congress Cataloging-in-Publication data:
Schultze, Charles L.
Other times, other places.
1. United States—Economic conditions—1945– .
2. Europe—Economic conditions—1945– . I. Title.
HC106.5.S378   1986   339'.0973   86-14759
ISBN 0-8157-7766-3
ISBN 0-8157-7765-5 (pbk.)

9 8 7 6 5 4 3 2 1

THE BROOKINGS INSTITUTION is an independent organization devoted to nonpartisan research, education, and publication in economics, government, foreign policy, and the social sciences generally. Its principal purposes are to aid in the development of sound public policies and to promote public understanding of issues of national importance.

The Institution was founded on December 8, 1927, to merge the activities of the Institute for Government Research, founded in 1916, the Institute of Economics, founded in 1922, and the Robert Brookings Graduate School of Economics and Government, founded in 1924.

The Board of Trustees is responsible for the general administration of the Institution, while the immediate direction of the policies, program, and staff is vested in the President, assisted by an advisory committee of the officers and staff. The by-laws of the Institution state: "It is the function of the Trustees to make possible the conduct of scientific research, and publication, under the most favorable conditions, and to safeguard the independence of the research staff in the pursuit of their studies and in the publication of the results of such studies. It is not a part of their function to determine, control, or influence the conduct of particular investigations or the conclusions reached."

The President bears final responsibility for the decision to publish a manuscript as a Brookings book. In reaching his judgment on the competence, accuracy, and objectivity of each study, the President is advised by the director of the appropriate research program and weighs the views of a panel of expert outside readers who report to him in confidence on the quality of the work. Publication of a work signifies that it is deemed a competent treatment worthy of public consideration but does not imply endorsement of conclusions or recommendations.

The Institution maintains its position of neutrality on issues of public policy in order to safeguard the intellectual freedom of the staff. Hence interpretations or conclusions in Brookings publications should be understood to be solely those of the authors and should not be attributed to the Institution, to its trustees, officers, or other staff members, or to the organizations that support its research.

Foreword

Most of the research aimed at finding predictable regularities in macroeconomic behavior, or illuminating some proposition in economic theory, examines the data for one country during one period—usually the years since World War II. In the three lectures that make up this book, Charles L. Schultze, a senior fellow in the Brookings Economic Studies program, compares several aspects of economic behavior in different historical eras and among different countries, and uses the similarities and differences to evaluate some current theoretical controversies and policy issues.

The first lecture compares the behavior of inflation in the United States in the last three decades with that in the years between the Civil War and World War I. From this comparison Schultze draws several conclusions about the nature of inflation and offers some views about its future prospects. The second lecture examines the behavior of real wages in the United States and four European countries during the recent past. Schultze questions the validity of the widely held view that real wages are more rigid in Europe than in the United States and that this rigidity explains the steady rise of European unemployment over the past ten years. The final lecture discusses the reasons that economic stability in the United States since World War II has been so much greater than it was in the late nineteenth and early twentieth centuries.

These lectures, delivered in October 1985, are part of a series established at Yale University in memory of Arthur M. Okun. In his preface to this book, James Tobin describes the series and notes the long, close relationship between Charlie Schultze and Art Okun, who was a senior fellow at Brookings from 1969 until his death in 1980.

The author wishes to thank Martin Neil Baily, Barry P. Bosworth, and George L. Perry for their advice and comments on early drafts of these lectures. Alan S. Blinder read the completed manuscript, made many valuable suggestions, and pointed out several errors that needed correction. Michael T. Thomas and Janet L. Chakarian provided excellent research assistance, Caroline Lalire edited the manuscript, Carolyn A. Rutsch checked it for factual errors, and Anita G. Whitlock typed the original manuscript and guided it through its many revisions. The underlying research was supported by a grant from the Ford Foundation.

The views in this book are solely those of the author and should not be ascribed to the Ford Foundation, to the persons whose assistance is acknowledged above, or to the trustees, officers, or other staff members of the Brookings Institution.

Bruce K. MacLaury
President

June 1986
Washington, D.C.

Contents

Preface

by James Tobin

Charles L. Schultze gave the second Arthur M. Okun Memorial Lectures at Yale University in October 1985. His three lectures are published here, as extended and revised.

The lecture series honors the memory of Arthur M. Okun (1928–80). The donor, a Yale alumnus who was a long-time associate, friend, and admirer of Okun, stated the reasons for the series in these words:

> Arthur Okun combined his special gifts as an analytical and theoretical economist with his great concern for the well-being of his fellow citizens into a thoughtful, pragmatic, and sustaining contribution to his nation's public policy.
>
> Extraordinarily modest personally, he was a delightful and trenchant activist on behalf of others—both as members of the whole society and as individuals. He touched many, many people in ways they will always cherish.
>
> Offered in affectionate appreciation of Art's gifts, this lecture series seeks to recognize and encourage professional economists to search for policies that will contribute to the betterment of life and living.

The first Okun lecturer, in October 1983, was Nicholas Kaldor. His lectures were published as *Economics without Equilibrium* (Armonk, N.Y.: M.E. Sharpe, 1985).

Art Okun's career, after his student years at Columbia, was divided among three institutions, to all of which he was deeply loyal: Yale, the Council of Economic Advisers, and the Brookings Institution.

Like Okun, Charlie Schultze has been an important figure in the Washington economic policy scene. He was a member of the CEA in the 1950s; in 1962 he became assistant director of the Bureau of the Budget; from 1965 through 1967 he was director of the Bureau. During the 1960s Art Okun was a member of the CEA and its chairman in the last two years of the Johnson administration. Thus Charlie and Art were close friends and colleagues in the Executive Office of the President, and then from 1969 at Brookings. In 1977 Charlie Schultze returned to the federal government as chairman of President Carter's Council of Economic Advisers, and we may be sure that he relied heavily on advice and help from Art, across town at Brookings.

It is obviously very fitting that Charlie Schultze give the Okun Lectures. It would be fitting even if Schultze and Okun had not enjoyed such close personal ties for so many years. Throughout his career Schultze has been an economist in the same spirit as Okun, the spirit that the lecture series seeks to honor and to perpetuate. Schultze has always looked for relevant facts and has dug deeply to find them. He has used theory and statistical technique not for their own sakes but as aids to common sense in organizing and understanding the facts. He has continually sought policies and institutions that would improve economic performance. The aspects of economic history and contemporary reality that he has tried to understand always have significant bearing on important issues of policy.

In these three Okun Lectures Schultze once again displays the qualities of his research. He resourcefully exploits U.S. data going back well into the nineteenth century, to help us understand inflation and its inertia, demand fluctuations and unemployment, and monetary policies and regimes. The policy motivation is to describe both the circumstances in which policies for demand stabilization can be constructively used and the limits to their use. He mobilizes data from several European countries to appraise the alleged diagnoses of their stagnation in the 1980s: structural unemployment and real wage rigidity. The moral is that the maladies are overstated, that they are not so severe that demand stimulus could not improve the economic performance of those economies. Finally, Schultze shows that the apparent improvement of U.S. macroeconomic performance since World War II, compared not only with the 1920s and 1930s but also with decades before World War I, is far from a statistical mirage. The trend real growth rate has been higher, and fluctuations have been less severe, with longer cyclical recoveries. Stabilization policies, of which both Schultze and Okun were expert and realistic practitioners, seem to have worked.

The publication of this volume by the Brookings Institution continues the cooperation between Brookings and Yale in undertakings honoring Arthur M. Okun. In September 1981 we both sponsored, together with Columbia University, a symposium in Okun's memory in New York. Brookings published the proceedings in *Macroeconomics: Prices and Quantities* in 1983. We at Yale are grateful to Brookings for publishing these lectures, too, and especially for lending us Charlie Schultze for a fruitful week, which included informal interchange with students and faculty as well as the lectures. It was fitting that Matthew Shapiro, who served on the CEA staff under Schultze and is now a faculty member at Yale, smoothly handled the logistics of the visit.

J.T.

June 1986
New Haven, Conn.

I

Inertial Inflation: Some Lessons from History

I was pleased but also a little awed when Jim Tobin asked me to deliver the second set of Arthur Okun Memorial Lectures. I am being asked to follow Nicholas Kaldor, whose Okun lectures in 1983 demonstrated once again that the time span of his intellectual creativity goes far beyond that given to most of us mortals. But I am particularly pleased and awed because of the person in whose memory these lectures are given. Art Okun was both a very dear friend and a long-time colleague of unique accomplishments.

Since my own research in recent years has dealt with the same subject that was at the center of Art Okun's attention for the last decade of his life—the relation between macroeconomic adjustment failures and the behavior of wages and prices in individual markets—I have had more occasion than most to recall and reflect on his work, especially its capstone, *Prices and Quantities*.[1] In preparing these lectures, I once again reviewed large parts of that book, including the chapter on asset prices to which I had originally paid less attention. I continue to be amazed at how much insightful yet rigorous analysis is crammed into almost every page, despite—I dare not say because of—the virtual absence of formal mathematical modeling.

The unifying theme in my three Okun lectures will be one of method rather than subject matter. I shall try to illuminate three

1. Arthur M. Okun, *Prices and Quantities: A Macroeconometric Analysis* (Brookings, 1981).

3

different areas of macroeconomic controversy by bringing to bear the insights gained from comparing and contrasting economic responses across different economic eras and among different countries. With, happily, a growing number of exceptions, most of the empirical work in support of macroeconomic theorems has been confined to an analysis of the time series for one country spanning at most the last three or four decades. I think understanding can be increased by extending the time span and enlarging the geographic coverage of the empirical analysis.

In the proper analytical framework, finding that economic responses to various kinds of shocks are similar over widely separated time periods or among different countries, despite differences in institutions, policy regimes, or historical experience, can help discriminate among alternative macroeconomic theories. Conversely, finding different responses over time or among countries invites a search for those differences in institutions, policy regimes, or historical experiences that can explain the contrasts in behavior.

In this lecture I first examine some empirical evidence bearing on the controversy about the nature of nominal wage behavior and the causes of inertial inflation that has exercised the economics profession over the past fifteen years. From an analysis of the behavior of inflation in the United States over more than a century, I suggest a role for the concept of rational expectations in an Okun-like model of inertial inflation. Having done that, I argue that the circumstances which gave rise to the macroeconomic problems of the 1970s and early 1980s, and which caused us to pay such a high price for inflation inertia, are in fact exceptional rather than typical of U.S. economic history. The economic problems that we are likely to face, and the macroeconomic controversies to which they are likely to give rise in the period ahead may have much less to do with wage and price behavior than has been the case in recent years.

In the second lecture I turn to the problem of the stickiness of real wages. I use comparative data for the United States and four European countries to evaluate the widely held view that while the United States suffers from nominal wage stickiness, Europe suffers from real wage stickiness, which in turn is the principal cause of its recent poor economic performance. I then offer a few tentative hypotheses about the reasons for the observed differences among countries in the way that wages and price-wage margins respond to economic shocks.

Finally, in the third lecture I return to the comparative analysis of the U.S. economy over the past century, and suggest several reasons for the improved stability of U.S. output and employment since the Second World War. Some recent work has challenged the validity of the data for the nineteenth and early twentieth century, suggesting that, the Great Depression aside, there has been little change over the past century in the stability of the U.S. economy. I therefore have to spend a little time on that empirical question.

The Short-Run Response of Inflation to Demand Shocks

There now exists almost an embarrassment of riches in the macroeconomic literature explaining why real and relative wages respond sluggishly to changes in the economic circumstances confronting individual firms. In a recent paper I grappled with the question that William Nordhaus keeps putting to us: why does real and relative wage stickiness imply nominal wage stickiness?[2] I sought to explain why the rational expectations of economic agents about the aggregate equilibrium wage level cannot provide a means of converting the real and relative wage stickiness of implicit contract literature into aggregate nominal flexibility. I shall not attempt to summarize those arguments here. For the purpose of these lectures I take their conclusions as given. But I do want to examine the implications of some empirical evidence that suggests how the rational use of information about the future is embodied in the conventions and rules of thumb that appear to govern the setting of wages and prices.

In its simplest terms the mainline approach to inflation analysis proceeds as follows: start with the concept of an underlying or expected rate of inflation. In the short run, actual inflation can be dislodged from the expected or underlying rate through changes in demand or supply conditions. In turn, if the changes in those conditions

2. Charles L. Schultze, "Microeconomic Efficiency and Nominal Wage Stickiness," *American Economic Review*, vol. 75 (March 1985), pp. 1–15.

and in actual inflation persist, they can bring about a long-run change and alter the initial underlying or expected rate.

Along these lines, the standard augmented Phillips curve, expressed in terms of price inflation, can conveniently be thought of as having three sets of components. First, there are the terms whose coefficients are determined by the slope of the short-period aggregate supply curve and relate the rate of inflation to the level, and changes in the level, of aggregate excess demand as measured by the ratio of actual to potential gross national product.[3] Second, there are supply-shock terms, whose coefficients embody the immediate effect on the inflation rate of shifts in the level of the aggregate supply curve induced by changes in terms of trade or other supply disturbances. And third, there is the term representing the underlying rate of inflation.

In the standard accelerationist version of the inflation process the third component of the inflation equation is interpreted as the prevailing expectation about the inflation rate held more or less in common by economic agents. Expectations adapt continuously and fully, but not necessarily quickly, to changes in actually experienced inflation. Thus the third set of terms in the standard Phillips curve equation is a distributed lag on past inflation rates whose coefficients sum to unity.

The Okun-Perry version of the inertial inflation process, on the other hand, interprets the underlying rate of inflation as deriving from a "norm" rate of wage increase that is implicitly accepted by firms and workers and that guides firms in their wage decisions. Payment of the norm wage increase is the neutral standard expected under the implicit contracts that dominate wage setting.[4] Payment of higher or lower than norm increases are made in response to demand and supply conditions, whose effect on inflation is captured in the first term of the equation. From a macroeconomic standpoint the most relevant

3. But the short-run aggregate supply curve referred to here should not be interpreted in the same way as the Lucas aggregate supply curve. In particular, it incorporates the view of firms as wage and price setters, and depicts the jointly determined response of both output and inflation to the level and changes in the level of excess aggregate demand. It is not based on modeling firms and workers as price takers, whose supply responses in competitive auctionlike markets would keep those markets on the verge of clearing except for (stochastic) mistakes in forecasting the general price level.

4. George L. Perry, "Inflation in Theory and Practice," *Brookings Papers on Economic Activity*, 1:1980, p. 216. (Hereafter BPEA.)

feature of the Okun-Perry norm is that it does not adapt fully and continuously to moderate changes in inflation that stay within normal cyclical experience. For workers and firms, maintenance of satisfactory long-term relations is a valuable asset to both.[5] Because it is difficult to judge whether moderate changes in inflation are ephemeral or permanent, and because payment of wages that do not conform to the norm are costly to the maintenance of long-term relations—even if sometimes necessary—the implicitly accepted norm tends to be relatively stable in the face of small changes in actual inflation. However, according to the Okun-Perry model, the norm does respond to large or sustained movements in actually experienced inflation. Ultimately norm inflation will adjust to a deviation of actual inflation from the norm, but such adjustments are not smooth and continuous.

There are thus two different ways in which inflation can be said to be sticky and characterized by inertia. First, the initial response of inflation to a change in aggregate demand may be relatively small, necessarily implying a relatively large response of output. And second, the feedback response of changes in actual inflation to changes in expected or norm inflation may be slow. In the standard accelerationist version of the Phillips curve, this response would be marked by a full and continuous but quite gradual adaptation of expected inflation to actual inflation experience. In the Okun-Perry version the response would show up as a substantially less than complete adaptation of the underlying inflation rate to small and temporary changes in inflation, with discrete shifts in the norm occurring in the face of large or long-sustained changes in actual inflation.

Both Robert Gordon and I have found that the coefficient on the first term—putatively reflecting the shallow slope of the short-run aggregate supply curve—has remained virtually unchanged in the United States during the peacetime years of the past century.[6] In an

---

5. Robert Hall estimated that in 1973 half of the work done in the United States was done on jobs in which workers could expect tenure of fifteen years or more. And if only adult male workers are considered, the relevant tenure is twenty-five years. Robert E. Hall, "Employment Fluctuations and Wage Rigidity," *BPEA, 1:1980*, pp. 91–123.

6. Robert J. Gordon, "A Consistent Characterization of a Near Century of Price Behavior," *American Economic Review*, vol. 70 (May 1980, *Papers and Proceedings, 1979*), pp. 243–49. The word *putatively* was inserted in this sentence to recognize the fact that in the new classical economics the observed slope of the short-run aggregate

Table 1-1. *Regression Equation of Annual Changes in U.S. Gross National Product Deflator, 1871–1914 and 1953–83*
Variables in percent except for dummies

Independent variable[a]	1871–1914		1953–83[b]	
	A	B	A	B
Constant	−2.14**	−2.34**	1.46**	0.61
$\hat{Q}^c$	0.22**	0.26**	0.25**	0.22**
$PDEV_{-1}$	...	−0.48**	d	d
p_{-1}	d	d	0.40**	0.86**
$(p_{imp} - p)_{-1}$	...	...	0.11**	0.09*
D_{1896}	3.98**	4.19**	...	...
D_{1968}	...	...	1.40**	...
D_{1974}	...	...	1.57*	...
Summary statistic				
$\bar{R}^2$	0.28	0.47	0.89	0.85
Standard error	2.98	2.55	0.79	0.90
Durbin-Watson	2.20	1.89	1.69	1.65

Source: Author's calculations.
* Significant at 10 percent level.
** Significant at 5 percent level.
a. $\hat{Q}$ = level of GNP relative to trend; p = change in GNP deflator; $(p_{imp} - p)$ = relative change in import prices; $PDEV$ = deviation of price level from trend (trend break in 1896); D_t = norm shift dummies.
b. For the years 1974–75 and 1979–81 the direct effect of changes in domestic energy prices is subtracted from the dependent variable. The years of Nixon price controls 1972–73, and the subsequent snapback 1974–75 were omitted from the regression. An alternative version with dummy variables for the price control years gives very similar results.
c. Sum of coefficients on $\hat{Q}$ and $\hat{Q}_{-1}$.
d. Insignificant; dropped in fitting equation (but see text).

equation using annual data for the overall economy, I found the sum of coefficients on the current and one-period lagged output ratio to have been the same in the postwar years 1953–83 as it was in the prewar period 1871–1914—about 0.25 (table 1-1). On this measure the short-run inertia of inflation was no less earlier than later. Indeed, the relative weight of the current year's lagged output ratio was greater in the postwar than in the prewar period, suggesting that the response now comes a bit quicker. But the annual data are not sufficiently sensitive to timing changes to make much of the last point.

In the short run, prices and nominal wages appear to move slowly

---

supply curve is not a structural parameter of the economic upturn but a variable that changes whenever the policy regime is changed.

and moderately around an implicitly accepted reference norm (or, if you will, around a set of prevailing expectations), and the magnitude of that short-run response has been little different in the postwar era than it was at the turn of the century.

In the earlier period a strict gold standard was in operation. The postwar era was one of managed money, in which the Federal Reserve attempted, in most recessions, to pursue an employment-supporting monetary policy. Both monetary regimes and the variance of nominal GNP changed sharply between the two periods. In the earlier period, for example, the standard deviation of both real and nominal GNP was 2.2 times its level in the postwar period. It is hard to square these facts with the propositions put forward by the new classical economics: that the slope of the short-run aggregate supply function is itself a variable which is heavily influenced by expectational patterns; and that it changes in response both to changes in the monetary policy regime and to the pattern of economic shocks.

The Longer-Run Response of Inflation

Although the short-run response of inflation to changes in aggregate demand have remained surprisingly stable between the early and the later periods, the long-run response is substantially different. There was no persistence effect during the early period. That is, an increase or decrease in inflation in one year did not exert an influence in the same direction on the inflation rate in the subsequent year.[7] The coefficient on the lagged dependent variable in the augmented Phillips curve equation was effectively zero. There is, in fact, some evidence to suggest that in the prewar period inflation expectations, or the inflation norm, were regressive on the price level. That is, whenever the price level rose above its trend path, it appeared to exert a negative influence on inflation in the next year. Thus when the deviation of the price level from its trend was entered in the equation, the coefficient on that term was significantly *negative* at four times its standard

7. This absence of a persistence effect in the prewar years is also found by Gordon, "A Consistent Characterization."

error. (This is the $PDEV_{-1}$ term in the second column of table 1-1.) Whenever the level of prices rose above trend by 1 percent, next year's price inflation tended to be pulled down by about 0.5 percent below what it otherwise would have been. A significant negative coefficient is also found when the regression is run for each of two subperiods, split at 1891.

There is, however, a potential downward bias to the coefficient on the $PDEV$ term and some danger that it may be a statistical artifact. By construction, a variable that is above trend must, except at the end of the period, come down to or below trend. And the shorter the period to which the trend is fitted, the more probable it is that the correction will occur the following year. But in the forty-four years of the prewar period only one trend break was inserted, in 1896. And, as noted earlier, a significant negative coefficient appears when the equation is fitted to each of the two subperiods. In the postwar years, with a single trend break either in 1968 or in 1973, a similar variable yielded small and insignificant coefficients. When three separate trend lines were used over the short space of thirty years, the deviation variable did yield a substantial negative coefficient, but then it was significant at the 5 percent level or better in only one of the two versions of the equation shown in table 1-1.[8] On balance, there was clearly no persistence effect in the formation of the inflation norm during the early period. As to whether prewar norm formation was regressive, the evidence has to be judged suggestive but not fully conclusive.

In contrast to its absence in the prewar period, a substantial persistence effect does appear in the behavior of inflation during the postwar years. A rise in actual inflation during one year is now at least partly reflected in a rise in the long-term inflation norm, or inflation expectations. There is some tendency to identify the persistence of inflation with the coefficient on the lagged dependent variable

8. When two breaks in the trend are inserted, giving three trend lines (1953–67, 1968–72, 1973–83), the coefficients (and t-statistics) on the $PDEV$ variable are: -0.31 (1.4) for the equation with dummy variables and -0.51 (2.9) for the equation without dummy variables. In contrast to the prewar period, however, when the postwar equations were fitted without the lagged inflation variable, the coefficient on the deviation variable was reduced to a small and insignificant number.

in an augmented Phillips curve equation and to conclude, mistakenly, that the appearance of such a persistence effect in the postwar years, contrasted with its absence earlier, implies that wages and prices were more flexible in the prewar period. Delong and Summers, in an otherwise enlightening paper on cyclical variability in the United States, make this interpretation of the evidence.[9] They then go on to suggest that the greater price flexibility in the prewar period was actually destabilizing and an important cause of the instability of output that characterized the period. But that is a wrong interpretation of the evidence. The data do *not* show that inflation exhibited the same equilibrium response to demand shocks in the two eras while doing so more slowly in the later one. Such evidence would indeed imply that aggregate price flexibility had declined. What the evidence actually shows is that the coefficient on the demand-shock term, representing the immediate response of inflation, was the same in the two periods. During the postwar era there was then a further response of inflation in subsequent years, as measured by the positive coefficient on the lagged dependent variable—a response that was absent in the earlier era. Thus, although the short-run response of wages and prices to a demand shock was the same in the two eras, the long-run response has become larger, not smaller, in the postwar years.

Estimates of the specific magnitude of the postwar persistence effect depend on the underlying model one uses to formulate the inflation equations. Equations that are based on the Okun-Perry model of the inflation process—employing dummy variables to capture nonlinear norm changes—give results which suggest that the inflation norm adapts only partially to moderate changes in actual inflation. For the postwar years this version is shown in the A column in table 1-1. Insofar as the coefficient on the lagged dependent variable is a reliable measure, about 40 percent of the actual change in inflation appears to be routinely incorporated in the norm. The conventions and rules of thumb governing changes in the norm under implicit contracts are apparently cautious ones. But large changes in inflation or sustained periods of excess demand, such as occurred in the United States in

9. J. Bradford Delong and Lawrence H. Summers, "The Changing Cyclical Variability of Economic Activity in the United States," Discussion Paper 1077 (Harvard University, Institute of Economic Research, August 1984).

the last four years of the 1960s, alter these conventions, and in response to such changes the norm adjusts more fully, giving rise to straight accelerationist behavior.

As might be expected, the augmented Phillips curve equations of the more conventional type, which do not allow for nonlinear shifts in the norm, show a larger persistence effect. As shown in the B column of the table, when the postwar norm shift dummies are dropped, the coefficient on the lagged dependent variable rises from 0.4 to 0.9.

On purely statistical grounds it is hard to choose between the two versions of the equation. One piece of evidence favoring the Okun-Perry version comes from some work by Edward Gramlich. In explaining consumers' expectations about inflation, as collected by the Michigan Institute for Social Research, he finds that the feedback from actual inflation to consumers' reported expectations takes on the same value—approximately 0.4—as does the feedback from actual inflation to the norm inflation rate in equations of the Okun-Perry.[10] Ultimately, however, one must rely on one's theoretical priors to choose between the two versions. In any event, the point I want to stress here is not the difference between these two alternatives but the fact that in the prewar period there was no persistence effect in the formation of the inflation norm, or of inflation expectations, whereas in the postwar period norm formation has shown a persistence effect whose magnitude may be in question but whose existence is clear.

The Relation between Rational Expectations and Norm Formation

The difference between the periods with respect to the persistence of inflation suggests a role for the concept of rational expectations in a model of sticky inflation. In that model the expectations of economic agents, rationally formed on the basis of prior experience, do not determine the short-run behavior of inflation—as in the new classical

10. Edward M. Gramlich, "Models of Inflation Expectations Formation: A Comparison of Household and Economic Forecasts," *Journal of Money, Credit, and Banking*, vol. 15 (May 1983), pp. 155–73.

economics—but do play a key role in shaping the generally accepted rules and conventions that govern the evolution of the inflation norm for purposes of wage setting.

In a world of long job tenures and unpredictable economic changes, wages (real, relative, and nominal) tend to be set in accordance with a body of social conventions and informal understandings that have been labeled implicit contracts. Under implicit contracts great store is set on wage decisions that appear fair and equitable in the context of prevailing wage norms or reference standards. To be a reasonable reference standard and not itself a source of conflict, the wage norm must reflect the basic facts of life as seen by economic agents. Norm formation in the years before World War I reflected the cyclical character of the period. The pattern of economic fluctuations from 1871 through 1914 was vastly different from what it has been in recent years. In the earlier period the standard deviations of annual changes in both real and nominal GNP were more than double what they were in the postwar years.[11] In the thirty-eight years from 1946 through 1983 there were no annual declines in real GNP as great as 2.5 percent. In the forty-four years from 1871 through 1914 there were six declines greater than 2.5 percent, averaging over 4 percent.

Not only the amplitude but the profile of the typical business cycles were different in the two periods. Between the end of the Civil War and the beginning of World War II the mean duration of contractions was almost the same as the duration of expansions—twenty-three and twenty-five months, respectively. After the war, contractions were shorter, eleven months on average, and expansions much longer, forty-six months (or thirty-three months if the very long expansion of the 1960s is excluded). The cycles of the period 1871–1914, measured in term of deviations from trend, thus took the form of deep Vs, with both sides of the V having equal length. In the postwar years the cycles took the form of a shallow check mark, with a long and gradually sloped right-hand stroke. Negative shocks were milder

11. Recently, in a series of papers (see note 1 in lecture 3), Christina Romer has argued that, in fact, most of the extant measures of output and employment in the early years overstate their variance and that cycles were not all that much larger than those of the postwar period. At the beginning of the third lecture I briefly present the arguments against Romer's conclusion.

and less persistent in the postwar period than they were earlier. Positive shocks were also milder, but they outlasted negative shocks by a ratio of 3½ or 4 to 1.

In the prewar period experience taught that expansions would not last long and were likely to be followed rather quickly by sizable contractions. Above-trend increases in the price level did not portend subsequent similar increases. Except for the one-time shift after 1896, there was no reason to believe that any changes in inflation above or below the prevailing norm were likely to persist. From 1871 through 1914 there were seventeen years in which the sign of the change in prices was opposite to that of the year before. What experience taught was that one year's rate of inflation had little to do with the next year's, except possibly as it may have raised or lowered the level of prices relative to the long-term trend, with a negative effect on subsequent inflation. And so in those years economic agents did not adjust their norm, or expected, inflation rate up or down in response to changes in actual inflation. The way the norm was formulated and adapted was thus rationally based on a long period of experience. Rational expectations came to be embodied in the particular social conventions and rules of thumb that underlay the formation of the reference norm in the implicit wage contracts of the time.

In World War II and in the first few postwar years the fear of a postwar depression and deflation was widespread. And in the recession of 1949 the GNP deflator did decline absolutely—though by only 1 percent. But as time went by, it gradually became evident that positive output shocks were likely to persist for a long time and negative shocks only briefly. One year of expansion was three to four times as likely to be followed by another year of expansion as by a contraction. It also became clear that declines in the average price level were unlikely and indeed that after a large rise prices would probably not stabilize at the new higher level, much less return to the old level, since the economic conditions associated with one year's price increase were more likely than not to be repeated the following year. As a result, in the forward-looking process of wage setting, the reference norm quite rationally came to be expressed as a continuing rate of inflation in prices and wages: this rate moved up or down, but cautiously and partially, in response to year-to-year changes in the actual inflation rate. Again, rational expectations shaped the conventions and rules of behavior underlying implicit contracts to conform to the experience of the postwar era. It is indeed likely that if the United States repeatedly went through an accelerationist period with continuing upward shifts in the norm, such as occurred during the late 1960s, the norm rate of inflation in implicit contracts would come to be adjusted upward much more quickly and fully in response to recently experienced inflation.

On the evidence offered from a comparison of the two periods, therefore, rational expectations about the course of the economy and the concept of regime changes have to be incorporated into the structuralist story of inertial inflation. Contrary to the view of the new classical economics, however, rational expectations do not enter as an element in explaining the short-term behavior of output and inflation. The observed short-run stickiness of wages and prices is a stable structural phenomenon and not an artifact of the interaction among market-clearing forces, a particular policy regime, and the pattern of demand shocks. Rational expectations enter as an element in explaining the longer-run response of inflation to economic changes. The nature and evolution of the implicitly accepted inflation norm around which short-run wage and price decisions are made is itself a rational reflection of the underlying patterns of the economic fluctuations that characterize the period. And when fundamental changes occur in that pattern—in the cyclical regime if you will—that change is gradually perceived and comes to be incorporated in the behavior of the inflation norm.

Economists are distinguished from other social scientists in that they have a commonly accepted criterion by which to judge any piece of economic analysis: namely, the extent to which it is consistent with rational maximizing behavior. But that should emphatically not mean that every component of macroeconomic theory must be modeled as the aggregation of individual actions and decisions by economic agents taken as the result of a continuous application of the maximizing calculus. There are, I think, some important aspects of economic life for which the calculus of rational maximization across stochastically distributed variables is an ill-suited tool to explain the day-to-day actions of economic agents. But that paradigm is often the appropriate technique for analyzing the source and the evolution of the conventions and rules of thumb that govern day-to-day actions and that form the basis for many of the macroeconomic regularities we observe. The economic rationale behind implicit labor contracts and the formation and evolution of the reference norms that are part of those contracts are important examples of this point.

The Macroeconomic Consequences of Nominal Wage and Price Stickiness

In *Prices and Quantities* Art Okun demonstrated that the stickiness of wage and price decisions is based on efficient microeconomic behavior, but that this microeconomic efficiency is purchased at a substantial cost in macroeconomic performance. The structural stickiness of individual wage and price movements radically weakens the link between changes in aggregate demand and changes in inflation while strengthening the links between demand and employment. The microeconomic hero is the macroeconomic villain. Okun had no trouble identifying the villain of the piece in the original Keynesian model. It was the wage floor, which he cited as Keynes' "basic explanation for persistent underemployment in slack, recession, or depression."[12] Okun replaced the Keynesian wage floor with the much richer concept of implicit labor contracts and customer product markets. For a downwardly rigid wage level he substituted a slowly adjusting rate of inflation. But as he saw it, the cause of the macroeconomic adjustment problem was fundamentally the same in both models—the failure of wages and prices to adjust promptly and fully to changes in aggregate demand.

Quite apart from the critique offered by the new classical economics, however, it is not at all clear that lack of wage and price flexibility is the universal source of macroeconomic adjustment problems. It is useful, in this context, to distinguish two categories of macroeconomic failure. The first is the failure of interest rates and other financial rationing devices to coordinate the intertemporal choices of savers

12. Okun, *Prices and Quantities*, p. 12.

and investors, and in particular to maintain aggregate demand at high levels in the face of sporadic downward shifts in the marginal efficiency of capital. The second is the failure of wages and prices to adjust promptly to clear markets in face of incipient declines in aggregate demand. In Keynes, the first failure is attributed to the effect of liquidity preference: with prices unchanged, interest rates cannot fall far enough to balance savings and investment at high-employment levels of income. If this initial failure to coordinate intertemporal choices of economic agents did not occur, there would be no need to rely on the painful mechanism of downward wage and price adjustment to create additional real money balances and so rescue the system from the shortage of aggregate demand created by the potential saving-investment imbalance.

Moreover, it is not self-evident that a high degree of wage and price flexibility would in fact produce the necessary change in real aggregate demand to offset the initial saving-investment mismatch. In the dynamics of the adjustment process a decline in the current inflation rate can generate a rise in the real interest rate. And if the positive effects on aggregate demand of the increase in real balances is smaller than the negative effects of the increase in real interest rates, the dynamic consequences of wage and price flexibility may generate more rather than less instability. Keynes himself took that view. Don Patinkin long ago emphasized this possibility.[13] In 1965 James Tobin sketched a model in which wage and price flexibility could be destabilizing.[14] And in a recent paper Bradford Delong and Lawrence Summers used vector autoregression results to argue that in both prewar and postwar years negative price shocks generated, at least for a while, negative output responses because of the effects of real interest rates.[15]

However this may be, it is, I think, incontrovertible that there are two sets of circumstances in which an inflation inertia of structural origin will necessarily give rise to serious macroeconomic failures, and in which the economy would be better off with wage and price

13. Don Patinkin, "Price Flexibility and Full Employment," *American Economic Review*, vol. 38 (September 1948), pp. 543–64.
14. James Tobin, "Money and Economic Growth," *Econometrica*, vol. 33 (October 1965), pp. 671–84.
15. Delong and Summers, "Changing Cyclical Variability."

flexibility. First, whenever an existing inflation has gone on long enough to become the underlying or norm rate, wringing out that inflation through the demand management tools available to modern governments will be very costly in terms of forgone output and employment. Second, to the extent the wage norm, despite its sluggishness, is shifted upward by the experience of a substantial increase in actual inflation, suppressing the longer-term inflationary consequences of large supply shocks will also cost dearly in terms of lost output and employment. When monetary policy is explicitly directed toward suppressing large supply shocks or wringing out an existing inflation, whatever its origins, the existence of inertia will necessarily generate large losses of output unemployment. They are precisely the circumstances that characterized the industrial world from the late 1960s through the early 1980s. And these are also the problems that occupied Art Okun in the last decade of his life and toward the better management of which his analysis and policy prescriptions were addressed.

Given the nature of the economic problems we experienced in those years, it is not surprising that the ferment in macroeconomics during most of that time centered on what determines microeconomic wage and price behavior. Though some older macroeconomic controversies continued, the main theoretical debate was over the causes of the observed inflation inertia—whether it stemmed from deep-seated and ineradicable structural causes, or rather from a pattern of expectations set in motion by faulty economic policies and remediable by better ones. Viewed in the light of earlier peacetime history, however, the period between the late 1960s and early 1980s was not typical. I think that the economic problems that will confront the nation and the theoretical controversies that will engage economists are likely to be quite different in the decade ahead.

The Special Character of the Period 1966–80

In the fifteen years from 1966 through 1980, the U.S. economy experienced three large inflationary shocks—first the Vietnam War boom and then the two OPEC oil shocks of 1974 and 1979–80. The first of these was endogenously generated from a major mistake in economic policy. Fueled in part by the failure to pay for the Vietnam War with a tax increase and by a monetary policy that was in the main accommodative, the economy was allowed to run at too frantic a pace for a very long time. The other two episodes were dominated by supply shocks imposed from the outside, principally the huge increases in oil prices. In 1972 and possibly in 1978 stimulative demand management policy also made some contribution to the increase in inflation. But as Otto Eckstein and Alan Blinder have argued with persuasive detail, the supply shocks were the principal moving force in the latter episodes.[16] Without them the increases in inflation would have been far smaller.

During the latter part of this fifteen-year period the trend of productivity growth slowed sharply. The empirical evidence suggests that the rate of inflation of money wages is not importantly influenced by the rate of productivity growth. The declining growth in productivity therefore tended to increase the growth in unit labor costs and price inflation rather than to lower the growth in money wages.

Each of the three main inflationary surges was followed by a recession, since macroeconomic policy permitted, and indeed fostered, a reduction in real aggregate demand to try to halt and then reverse the spread of inflation. After the inflationary episodes of the late 1960s and 1973–74, the rapid rise in unemployment led to a fairly quick reversal of policy, even though the underlying inflation rate had not been pulled down to where it had been before the inflationary episode began. Finally, beginning in 1980 and intensifying in 1981, the restraint on demand was made ruthless enough and maintained long enough for it, together with favorable changes in oil and import prices, to bring the underlying inflation rate down from 10 to 4 percent, about two-thirds of the way to where it had been in the mid-1960s.

The disappointing economic profile of the period 1966–80 was thus shaped by economic policy sporadically trying to stop and then reverse three large inflationary shocks when—because of inflation

16. Otto Eckstein, *Core Inflation* (Prentice-Hall, 1981); and Alan S. Blinder, "The Anatomy of Double-Digit Inflation in the 1970s," National Bureau of Economic Research Conference Paper 95 (Cambridge, Mass.: NBER, 1981).

inertia—the main tool available, demand restraint, could purchase inflation control or reduction only at very high costs in output and employment. I am not trying to suggest that if the three inflationary shocks had not occurred, no other macroeconomic adjustment problems would have been encountered. But those shocks, and the policy responses to them, dominated the period. A reading of American economic history suggests, however, that the particular conditions which plagued the United States and the world economy during those years and which gave rise to this profile were unprecedented in character and magnitude.

In the United States the rise in inflation and in the inflation norm that began in the last half of the 1960s came in response to a uniquely large and long period of excess demand. By the end of 1965 the then current economic expansion had already been under way for longer than any peacetime expansion since the Civil War. Four more years of very high aggregate demand were then tacked on to that expansion. By 1966 the Perry-weighted unemployment rate had been pushed down to 2.6 percent, where it remained for the remaining four years of the expansion.[17] As estimated by Robert Gordon, the American economy in each of those four years operated between 4 and 5 percent above its potential.[18] And during the same period manufacturing output ranged between 87 and 91 percent of capacity, a level otherwise reached in only two single years in the postwar period.

Although, as I argued earlier, the norm rate of inflation does not fully adjust in an accelerationist way to changes in demand and actual inflation that are within typical cyclical bounds, an expansion of this length and strength clearly went beyond those bounds. Inflation did not accelerate during the first six years of the 1960s, but did so with a vengeance starting in 1966. The unemployment rate—either as conventionally measured or as adjusted by Perry—remained at about the same very low level for four years, but inflation, as measured by the private nonfarm deflator, rose steadily from 1.5 percent in 1965 to 3 percent in 1967 to 5 percent in 1970. The length of the expansion, the strength of demand, and the sustained rise in inflation were without

17. Charles L. Schultze, "Some Macro Foundations for Micro Theory," *BPEA*, 2:1981, p. 557.
18. Gordon, "A Consistent Characterization."

parallel in our peacetime history, at least since the Civil War, and were clearly such as to break through the relative stability of the inflation norm and drive it up to a significantly higher level.

The magnitude of each of the two supply shocks in the 1970s was also far outside the historical range of other supply shocks to the American economy. In the first shock both food and energy prices rose steeply. The second shock was mainly confined to energy prices, but the energy price rise was larger than in the first shock. I have elsewhere estimated that the upward shift in the level of the aggregate supply curve for consumer goods—not including any indirect effect on wages—amounted to about 5 percent in the first shock and 6 percent in the second. The data are not available to make the same calculations for the years before World War II. But an examination of prices for energy and for raw materials clearly indicates that nothing of a similar magnitude occurred. In the six-year period from 1897 through 1902, rising relative prices of farm products may have added about 1.5 percent a year to the GNP deflator, and some of that was probably a demand rather than a supply phenomenon. There is nothing comparable to the sharp supply shocks of 1973–74 and 1979–80.

The same structural aspect of the economy that caused so much trouble in the recent past—the sluggishness of the inflation response to aggregate demand—may turn out to be helpful in the period ahead. If the American economy does not painlessly retreat from inflation, neither does it easily generate an increase in inflation. The short-run response of inflation to higher demand is modest, and the underlying inflation norm or, if you will, the state of inflationary expectations does not adjust upward fully and promptly in the face of moderate increases in actual inflation. Inflation in the United States is not on a hair-trigger release. Small mistakes of policy or supply shocks of modest size should not inaugurate a new upward shift in the inflation norm. Because of the large costs of eliminating an increase in inflation once it has become embedded in the norm, we need to exercise continuing caution about the speed and extent of aggregate demand expansion. But insofar as both our theoretical debates and our policy controversies in the last fifteen years developed in response to a series of atypical economic events, we may well find both theoretical controversies and policy concerns sharply changing in the period ahead.

No one can give guarantees against large new supply shocks in the decade ahead. A political upheaval in the Middle East might conceivably reverse the current weakness in oil prices. If the overvaluation of the dollar should disappear and the dollar overshoot on the downside with a speculative rush, the U.S. aggregate supply curve could, for a time, shift up rapidly. And finally, the continuation of large structural budget deficits in the United States, combined with a shrinkage in the inflow of foreign savings, might conceivably put such pressure on the Federal Reserve that it would finance an expansion in aggregate demand large enough to start a new round of higher inflation. These are all possible scenarios. But they are not, I think, probable ones. Inflation will rise somewhat from its very low level in 1985 as the dollar declines. But with a little luck and only average good sense and political courage in managing our monetary affairs, the decade ahead should not see a repetition of the circumstances that shaped the profile of the 1970s. We may therefore find ourselves shifting the focus of the macroeconomic policy debate. When the implicit, or explicit, goal of monetary policy was to shrink the existing growth rate of nominal GNP, either to reduce a continuing inflation or to prevent a one-time supply shock from becoming a new wage-price spiral, the downward resistance of wage and price inflation to economic slack was almost by definition the one source of increased unemployment and output loss. And greater flexibility of wages and prices would obviously have been a macroeconomic boon. But macroeconomic instability and underemployment are not always due to the clash of disinflationary monetary policy with the structural inertia of inflation. The particular circumstances confronting the world industrial economies in the 1970s may have caused us to concentrate too exclusively on sticky wages and prices as the principal source of macroeconomic ills.

It is not my intent in these lectures to discuss the kinds of macroeconomic adjustment problems and analytical challenge that are likely to claim our attention in the period ahead. There are a few broad themes, however, that seem to me to be emerging.

In the last few years substantial imbalances have arisen between the high-employment levels of domestic national savings and domestic investment opportunities in major industrial countries, with the United States moving in one direction and Japan and Europe in another. Both private investment trends and governmental policies have helped to generate these imbalances. Macroeconomic developments have become less explainable by the clash between inertial inflation and deflationary economic policy, and increasingly dominated by the changes in interest rates and exchange rates and the reshuffling in capital and trade flows that have occurred as the world's economies responded to the appearance of these imbalances.

In the United States, after a short but eventful period in which the Federal Reserve adopted monetarism as a political cover for undertaking the painful task of disinflation, the Fed in 1982 effectively switched from monetary targeting to a policy of managed money, aimed at achieving a set of performance goals largely defined by the growth of aggregate demand. I think that now the Fed's main targeting objective is to set upper and lower limits to the growth of real aggregate demand. It has other goals, but I think it gives chief weight at the present time to the objective I have described. To a first approximation, and subject to some constraints having to do with the presence or absence of outside inflationary shocks, one can think of the short-run operation of monetary policy as endogenous: it provides a flow of bank reserves consistent with keeping aggregate demand from wandering outside an upper and a lower set of limits. If the Federal Reserve is successful, and if the constraints do not become binding, the main effects for the U.S. economy of the international saving-investment imbalances will be on the structure and composition of output and employment rather than on their aggregate levels.

From an analytical standpoint, both the outcome of monetary policy actions and the direction of structural changes in the economy will be heavily influenced by relationships about which we currently know far too little. The first of these, of course, is the determinants of real exchange rates, and particularly the relation between changes in portfolio balances among currencies and the demand for those currencies. The second is the effect of the 1970s financial deregulation on the elasticity of domestic demand for investment and other durable goods to changes in interest rates and other financial rationing devices. And a less important but interesting third is the effect of that financial deregulation in changing the slope and stability of the demand function for transaction balances, and the consequences of those changes for the short-run operation of monetary policy. In the coming years these analytical questions and the effect of savings-investment imbalances on the structure of aggregate demand may concern us much more than the causes and consequences of inertial inflation.

II

Real Wage Rigidity in Europe: Reality or Illusion?

The first lecture dealt with some of the causes and consequences of one kind of failure of macroeconomic coordination—the stickiness of nominal wages. In recent years a new literature has bloomed that deals with a related but different problem— the stickiness of real wages. This kind of market failure has been widely identified as an important source of Europe's poor economic performance during recent years, often called Eurosclerosis.

In this lecture I consider the behavior of real wages in the United States and in Europe, their relation to macroeconomic performance, and some of the microeconomic reasons for the observed differences in their behavior. I proceed in three steps. First, I examine the extent to which European real wages are in some sense too high. Next, using simulation results from equations explaining nominal wages and the margin of prices over wages, I compare and contrast how nominal wages, price-wage margins, and hence real wages respond to various kinds of economic shocks. Finally, I speculate on some of the possible microeconomic reasons for the differences in responses among countries.

European Economic Performance since 1973

In the decade after 1973 the unemployment rate in both Europe and the United States rose substantially. But the two regions contrasted sharply in the way unemployment changed over time. In the United States there were large cyclical swings around the longer-term trend of unemployment, including a substantial decline in the unemployment rate after its 1982 peak. Though almost everyone concludes that some of the increase in U.S. unemployment has been structural and cannot be eliminated simply by an expansion of demand, much of the worsening average performance was attributable to the depth and duration of the last two recessions, 1974–75 and 1981–82. In Europe, by contrast, the rise in unemployment was unremitting and accelerated after 1980. Between 1974 and 1984 the European unemployment rate increased in every year save one (and in that one year unemployment simply stopped rising, it did not fall). Moreover, in most European countries a much larger proportion of unemployment is of long duration than in the United States. In 1983, for example, 24 percent of the U.S. unemployed had been out of work for longer than six months. In Germany that proportion was 54 percent; in the United Kingdom, 58 percent; in France and the Netherlands, almost 70 percent; and in Belgium, 78 percent.[1]

The longer average duration and apparent cyclical insensitivity of the unemployment increase in Europe has led many economists on both sides of the Atlantic to conclude that the rise in European unemployment is largely structural and hence is not curable by an expansion in aggregate demand. The widespread acceptance of this view by European political leaders helps explain the cautious macro-economic policies that have characterized most European countries since the late 1970s. A large expansion of demand, it is believed, would soon lead not to sustained gains in output and employment but to higher inflation.

Though many structural causes have been cited for the rise in European unemployment, which largely involve various kinds of rigidities in the European labor markets, the most dominant view is that European real wages are too high and downwardly rigid. There is no question that during the 1970s European real wages rose substantially faster than the growth in labor productivity for the four countries I examined. In comparing 1978–80 with 1968–70, the

1. *OECD Observer*, no. 130 (September 1984), p. 6.

excess of the growth in real wages over the growth in productivity in the manufacturing sector is as follows: United Kingdom, 10.3 percent; West Germany, 13.3 percent; Sweden, 13.5 percent; and Italy, 9.2 percent.[2]

For the economy as a whole or for a given sector of the economy, it is arithmetically true that labor's share of income will rise or fall (and the profit share move in the opposite direction) depending on whether the increase in real product wages is faster or slower than the increase in labor productivity. By the term *real product wages* I mean the ratio of nominal wages to value-added prices. When the growth of productivity slows, the growth of real product wages must also slow to avoid a shift in income shares from profits toward labor. The growth of *real purchasing power wages*—the ratio of nominal wages to consumer prices—will be the same as the growth of real product wages when consumer prices and value-added prices are moving together. But a change in the terms of trade associated, for example, with a rise in imported oil prices will cause consumer prices to move differently from domestic value-added prices. Should a deterioration in the terms of trade occur, the growth of nominal wages must slow relative to consumer-price inflation—the path of real purchasing power wages must be adjusted downward if a shift in income shares away from profits is to be prevented. There are thus several widely used measures of excess real wage growth in Europe. The first is the change in labor's share of income over some base period. Alternatively, the same measure can be constructed by taking the cumulative excess of the growth in real product wages over the growth in labor productivity, or what is again approximately the same thing, the cumulative excess of the growth in real purchasing power wages over the growth of productivity, adjusted for changes in the terms of trade. All these roughly equivalent measures have been labeled the *real wage gap*.

Because of their downward rigidity, European real purchasing power wages, it is said, did not make the appropriate adjustment to the large rise in oil prices and the decline in productivity growth that

2. Real wages are nominal compensation per hour divided by the price of output originating in the manufacturing sector.

occurred in the 1970s. As a result, the growth in real product wages during that period was larger than warranted by the fundamentals of productivity growth and terms of trade. Moreover, the excess rise in real wages came on top of an earlier, exogenous wage explosion that occurred in most countries in Europe in the last years of the 1960s and that pushed up real as well as nominal wages.[3] A large gap between actual and warranted real wages opened up and was perpetuated. Labor's share of income rose and profits were squeezed.

The very high level of real wages and their downward rigidity are said to have produced structural unemployment and to have limited the possibility of output expansion in several ways. First, faced with the high level of real wages, European firms have intensified the rate at which capital is substituted for labor along long-run production functions, thereby raising unemployment.[4] This process the Organization for Economic Cooperation and Development (OECD) calls labor displacement. Even though the consequent increase in productivity has in the last several years lowered the ratio of real wages to productivity and reduced labor's share of income, the current level of real wages is still too high to allow full employment of the existing labor force.

Second, employers are operating on their notional short-run demand curves for labor. They can sell all the output they are willing to produce, but they will not expand output because, given the level of real wages, it is unprofitable for them to bring back into operation higher-cost units of currently unused capacity. They have reduced their work force and idled less profitable units of capital, a process the OECD calls labor shedding.[5] Output will not rise unless real wages fall. But workers' insistence on maintaining an excessively high path of real wages means that any fiscal or monetary stimulus engenders higher wage inflation rather than lower real wages and increased

---

3. I call the wage explosion of 1968–70 exogenous in the sense that it did not appear to be generated either by a large excess demand for labor or a price-raising supply shock. See George L. Perry, "The Determinants of Wage Inflation around the World," *Brookings Papers on Economic Activity*, 2:1975, pp. 403–05; and Jeffrey D. Sachs, "Wages, Profits, and Macroeconomic Adjustment," *BPEA*, 2:1979, pp. 277–80.

4. *OECD Economic Outlook*, vol. 37 (June 1985), p. 30.

5. Ibid.

output. The resulting unemployment has been called classical unemployment.

Third, from a longer-term standpoint, the profit squeeze has discouraged capacity-expanding investment, so that higher employment of the labor force has become increasingly inconsistent with the availability of capacity. Even if the real wage rigidity were now relaxed, expansion would quickly run into capacity bottlenecks.[6]

Two related but distinct propositions are involved in the real wage explanation of Europe's economic problems. The first proposition is that the level of European real wages has been and still is excessive; the second is that the problem stems from the nature of the wage-setting institutions in Europe that produce downwardly rigid real wages—real wages do not adjust downward to reflect slowdowns in productivity growth or supply shocks. I want to discuss each of these propositions in turn.

The Real Wage Gap

Because of the lack of adequate European data on average wage rates for the entire economy, almost all the comparative analysis of the real wage gap has been done with manufacturing data. For this reason, it is not generally appreciated that in most European countries labor's share of income for the total economy rose only moderately; only in manufacturing did labor's share rise very much (table 2-1).[7]

Because of the lack of economy-wide wage data, I also restricted my analysis to the manufacturing sector. The first task in analyzing the behavior of real wages relative to changes in productivity is to eliminate the influence of cyclical changes in productivity. To do this, I estimated the trend growth in productivity from an equation, originally developed by Peter Clark. The equation assumes that the

6. Edmund Malinvaud, *The Theory of Unemployment Reconsidered* (Wiley, 1977).

7. Later in this lecture I present evidence indicating that real wages in manufacturing are very sensitive to real exchange rates in several European countries. The influence of exchange rates on real wages in service and other industries producing nontradable goods is presumably much less. This may explain part of the divergence between the behavior of labor's share of income in manufacturing and in the overall economy.

Table 2-1. *Labor's Share of Income in the Total Economy and Manufacturing in Seven Countries, Selected Years and Periods, 1960–83*
Percent

Category	1960	1961–73	1974–81	1981	1982	1983
Total economy[a]						
United States	74	73	74	73	74	74
United Kingdom	72	73	75	75	74	73
West Germany	71	72	73	73	72	71
Sweden	n.a.	n.a.	n.a.	n.a.	n.a.	n.a.
Italy	81	80	83	84	83	86
France	73	72	75	76	76	75
Japan	82	74	81	81	82	82
Manufacturing						
United States	71	70	73	75	76	73
United Kingdom	68	72	80	81	78	76
West Germany	55	58	65	68	67	64
Sweden	66	72	78	80	76	68
Italy	51	57	64	62	62	64
France	59	61	66	67	66	65
Japan	39	42	51	50	50	51

Sources: Total economy data from Commission of the European Communities, *European Economy*, vol. 22 (November 1984), table 24; manufacturing data from author's calculations based on U.S. Bureau of Labor Statistics data.
n.a. Not available.
a. The labor share includes an imputed share of labor income of unincorporated proprietors as estimated by the staff of the Commission of the European Communities.

actual hours of labor input adjust gradually to a target level that itself depends on output, the ratio of output to its potential, and the trend path of productivity growth.[8] My estimates allowed for several changes in the trend that the data seemed to dictate. I then constructed a measure of the so-called real wage gap, based on the trend path of productivity extracted from this equation. Finally, I estimated that gap for the United States and four European countries—the United Kingdom, West Germany, Sweden, and Italy.

By 1983 the adjusted real wage gap in the United States, relative to a 1963–68 base period, had risen above the wage gap in the three continental countries (table 2-2).[9] Similarly, Robert Gordon found that by 1983 the cyclically adjusted wage gaps in the United States

8. Peter K. Clark, "Productivity and Profits in the 1980s: Are They Really Improving?" *BPEA*, 1:1984, pp. 133–67.
9. See also note b to table 2-2.

Table 2-2. *Manufacturing Wage Gaps in Five Countries, 1956–83*[a]
Percentage points

Period or year	United States	United Kingdom[b]		West Germany	Sweden[b]	Italy
1956–60	1.2	−1.4		−3.2	−4.2	−5.0
1961–65	1.2	0.2		0.6	−2.0	−0.7
1966–70	−0.6	0.3		−0.4	1.7	0.6
1971–75	2.4	4.1		1.8	2.7	7.5
1976–80	4.1	7.9	(7.5)	6.8	8.7	7.6
1981	5.6	8.4	(9.9)	8.6	7.2	5.6
1982	7.1	6.2	(9.1)	6.3	3.5	3.5
1983	5.8	5.7	(10.2)	4.5	1.1	3.2

Source: Author's calculations.

a. The wage gap measures the percentage-point change in labor's share of income, relative to a 1963–68 base period, due to the excess of the growth of real product wages over the trend growth of productivity.

b. The wage gap in the United Kingdom is substantially larger than in all other countries during 1981–83 if the productivity equation does not include a trend shift in 1981. The t-statistic on the upward shift in trend was 1.5. The numbers in parentheses show the wage gaps for the United Kingdom calculated without a shift in productivity trend in 1981. Continued substantial gains in productivity in 1984 in the United Kingdom (4.5 percent) suggest that the recent trend shift is real.

and Japan were much greater than those in nine out of eleven European countries he examined—only Austria and Norway had larger wage gaps than the United States.[10] In contrast to Japan and the United States, most European countries by 1983 had substantially reduced the gap that had earlier opened up between real product wages and adjusted productivity, relative to a pre-1970 base period. Thus the most successful recoveries from the 1981–82 recession came in those countries whose adjusted wage gaps were the largest. In Europe, unemployment has continued to rise since 1981 while the wage gap has shrunk.

It has been argued that the recent decline of the wage gap in Europe does not imply a diminishing real wage problem. According to this view, the excess rise in real wages during the late 1970s had a lagged effect in accelerating the substitution of capital for labor, which in turn raised productivity and created additional unemployment but also reduced the measured wage gap. At existing real interest rates, wages are still too high to be compatible with full employment of the

10. Robert J. Gordon, "Wage-Price Dynamics and the Manufacturing Output Gap in Europe, Japan, and North America," paper presented at the Conference on Unemployment, Yxtaholm, Sweden, September 26–27, 1985.

labor force. On this line of reasoning the fall in the wage gap in many European countries since 1981 is, paradoxically, a consequence of excess real wages. If the recent decline in the wage gap were indeed a result of the earlier excessive rise in real produced wages, there should be a substantial negative association between the extent of the slowdown in productivity in a country and the increase in its wage gap. Gordon has measured manufacturing wage gaps for eleven European countries. A cross-country correlation based on those estimates produces only a small and insignificant negative coefficient when the slowdown in productivity growth since 1972 is regressed on the magnitude of the rise in the wage gap.[11] Direct estimates of changes in productivity growth in manufacturing induced by changes in capital-labor intensity show that such induced growth rose in Belgium and Norway (as implied by the excess real wage hypothesis) but fell in Germany and Italy and was approximately unchanged in France and Sweden.[12]

Besides the recent contrasting behavior of real wages in Europe and the United States, there are several other reasons to be skeptical of the argument that rigid real wages now inhibit European expansion. In the first place, the rise in labor's share of income in the manufacturing sector started much earlier than the 1970s: it began in the late 1950s or early 1960s and continued through the period of very rapid European growth. This rise in real wages relative to average productivity growth did speed up substantially during the 1970s, when gains in real purchasing power wages failed to decline promptly in the face of increases in imported oil prices and slowing productivity growth. But if the longer-term trend is taken into account, the excess growth of real wages that opened up in the 1970s is less striking than it

11. Ibid., tables 3 and 4. The change in trend productivity growth after the fourth quarter of 1972 was correlated with the change in the cyclically adjusted wage gap between 1971–73 and 1981. The coefficient on the independent variable was -0.04 (1.1); $\bar{R}^2 = 0.03$.

12. James Chan-Lee and Helen Sutch have estimated the growth of total factor productivity for a number of European countries. "Profits and Rates of Return," *OECD Economic Studies*, no. 5 (Autumn 1985), table 5, p. 151. Subtraction of the growth of total factor productivity from the growth of average labor productivity gives the increase in labor productivity due to changes in the ratio of capital to labor. There is an apparent error in one component of the estimate for the United States, which makes it impossible to draw a conclusion.

appears in the raw data, markedly so in Sweden and Italy but also somewhat in Germany and the United Kingdom.

The OECD has published gross operating rates of return on capital stock and gross profit shares for the manufacturing sectors of a number of European countries for selected dates. For the four countries of my study, I adjusted those estimates to eliminate cyclical swings in productivity growth and in the ratio of capital to output. The adjusted rates of return in most countries were very high around 1960. They fell substantially through the 1960s and into the early 1970s and moved down much more slowly thereafter. The fall in the profit rate from its very high level in the early postwar years and the rise in the labor share from its very low level suggest that some of the change in income shares that we have witnessed may have been a natural consequence of growth. In the 1950s and early 1960s Europe experienced a capital scarcity. The technological frontier was far ahead of average practice in most European manufacturing firms. Rates of return on investment in manufacturing were abnormally high relative to the cost of capital, inducing a large and long-lasting investment boom that greatly increased capital intensity. As would be expected, that process drove down the initially high rates of return on the manufacturing capital stock.

If the elasticity of factor substitution in manufacturing is less than one—as some research has indicated—the movement toward a new equilibrium involving a large increase in the capital-labor ratio would raise both the marginal product of labor and real wages faster than the average product of labor. The labor share would rise. If so, what we have witnessed in Europe by way of a rising labor share and a falling profit rate was in part a movement from disequilibrium to equilibrium rather than vice versa. The phenomena associated with the process I have described can be clearly seen in the data for Japan, and to a lesser extent Germany and Italy, shown in table 2-1. In these three countries the labor share in manufacturing rose throughout the 1960s and the 1970s. But the rise started from a very low level, and much of it had taken place by the mid-1970s. In Japan the 1960 labor share was only 39 percent. By 1980 or 1981, after a long period of large increases in the capital-labor ratio, the manufacturing labor shares in the three countries were still below those in the United States and the United Kingdom—in the Japanese case far below. This suggests a world in which an initial capital scarcity, characterized by high profit rates and relatively low labor shares, was gradually eased by heavy investment.

To test the proposition that a substitution elasticity of less than one might have produced rising labor shares in association with increasing capital-output ratios, I fit for the four European countries—the United Kingdom, Germany, Italy and Sweden—a pooled cross-section and time-series regression of the manufacturing gross profit rate on the cyclically adjusted capital-output ratio. The regression included a time trend with a linear spline in 1974 and a dummy variable for Italy to reflect the belief that its set of technological opportunities was lower than that of other countries. If the European countries are operating at different stages along the same basic set of production opportunities, if the underlying production function has a constant elasticity of substitution, and if the average rate of return on the capital stock can be assumed to be equal to the marginal product of capital, one can identify the common elasticity of factor substitution from the first-order conditions—that is, from the regression of the profit rate on the capital-output ratio. The elasticity of substitution so calculated was indeed significantly less than one—namely, 0.72. Thus in the normal course of events the large increases in capital intensity that took place in Europe in the 1950s and 1960s were accompanied by increases in labor's share of income.

This finding does not, of course, exclude the possibility that European real wages are too high and too rigid to be compatible with a return to high employment. By no means all the change in the labor share was due to this growth process, especially in Germany and the United Kingdom. Nevertheless, the finding does demonstrate that one cannot measure the extent of excess real wages simply by comparing the current labor share to its value in some pre-1970 base period.

Short-Run Determinants of Changes in Real Wages

There is another major problem with the evidence usually adduced to demonstrate that downward real wage rigidity characterizes the

European economies—a problem that Gordon has also noted.[13] One cannot simply point to the existence of a large coefficient on lagged consumer prices in a wage equation and conclude that real wages are sticky. Wage bargains, even in Europe, do not get instantly renegotiated as prices change unexpectedly. Even if the coefficient of wage changes on recent prior price changes is large, increases in aggregate demand could still lower real wages so long as nominal wages were set for some period, say a year, while prices responded quickly to changes in demand conditions. Even more important, wage bargains do not determine real wages. Rather, how prices respond to changes in wages and to many other economic events is equally important in the development of real wages.

If the level of prices were quickly and fully adjusted to cover changes in unit labor costs, the behavior of nominal wages in response to supply shocks would largely determine the rate of inflation but not the level of real wages. In fact, from a macroeconomic standpoint the behavior of prices relative to wages is complex, responding in different ways to different kinds of changes in macroeconomic variables. Consider, for example, a decrease in the ratio of actual GNP to potential GNP. The associated rise in unemployment should, after a time, begin to lower the rate of nominal wage increases. But the magnitude and even the direction of the subsequent changes in real wages depend on how prices respond. How quickly are those changes in labor costs reflected in prices? To what extent and how quickly are markups influenced by the growth of unused capacity? As domestic prices begin to change, how much of the change shows up in subsequent wage changes and how quickly? With domestic prices of tradables changing relative to foreign prices, does the nominal exchange rate fully and promptly adjust to keep the real exchange rate constant? If not, how much does the resulting movement in the real exchange rate affect domestic price-wage margins? Does the real exchange rate respond differently to fiscal shocks than it does to monetary shocks? The magnitude and timing of all these effects will determine the course of real wages in response to an exogenous sustained change in the output ratio (the ratio of actual to potential output). Similarly complex

13. Gordon, "Wage-Price Dynamics."

chain reactions will occur in response to other economic events. It is obviously impossible to draw conclusions about the rigidity or flexibility of real wages on the basis of one or even several coefficients in a wage equation. Thus the OECD's recent measure of real wage rigidity—the ratio of the coefficient on lagged prices to the coefficient on unemployment in a standard wage equation—is not particularly useful.

I have completed an analysis of these relationships for the manufacturing sectors of the United States and the four countries whose production function I discussed earlier—the United Kingdom, Germany, Sweden, and Italy. Let me summarize them here. For each of the five countries I estimated separate equations for nominal wages and for price-wage margins over the period 1964–83. For the United States I also estimated the same equations for the private nonfarm sector as a whole. I then simulated the effects of various kinds of shocks on real and nominal wages.

The following is the basic equation for wage inflation (period of fit, 1964–83):

$$(2\text{-}1) \quad w_t = a_0 + a_1\hat{q} + a_2\hat{Q}_{-1} + a_3p^v_{-1} + a_4(p^c - p^v)_{-1} + a_5D,$$

where

w = rate of change in hourly compensation
$\hat{q}$ = change in output relative to trend
$\hat{Q}$ = level of output relative to trend
p^v = rate of change in value-added prices
p^c = rate of change in the personal consumption deflator
D = a norm shift dummy.

Several features of the equation should be noted. First, in the wage equations, following the methodology discussed in the first lecture, I included a dummy variable for a shift in the inflation norm, which occurred at the end of the 1960s or the beginning of the 1970s (the precise date varied with each country). This shift in the norm was insignificant in Sweden, but significant in the four other countries.[14]

14. In Germany the dummy variable took on a value different from zero only in 1969 and 1970. That is, the wage explosions of 1969–70 did not, in Germany, permanently shift up the inflation norm. For the United States the years 1972–75,

Following a theoretical rationale worked out by Robert Gordon, I next separated consumer price inflation into two components— changes in the price of value added for domestic manufactured goods, and the difference between the change in that price index and the change in consumer prices.[15] It is importantly supply shocks, such as large changes in the relative price of oil or other imports, that cause the change in consumer prices to differ from the change in value-added prices. Thus the wage equation was designed to determine whether changes in firms' own value-added prices influence wages differently from supply shocks or other influences that change consumer prices relative to manufacturing value-added prices.

A fit of these wage equations to the period 1964–83 confirms the widely held view that the short-run response of U.S. nominal wages to economic slack (as measured by $\hat{Q}$), in both the private nonfarm economy as a whole and in the manufacturing sector, was much smaller than the wage response in the manufacturing sector of all four European countries (table 2-3). But the response of nominal wages in U.S. manufacturing both to changes in value-added prices and to the other elements changing consumer prices was larger than it was in the U.S. nonfarm sector as a whole and in the European countries except the United Kingdom.

It has been widely recognized that in the late 1960s and in the 1970s U.S. manufacturing wages rose relative to other wages. This relative increase closely coincided with the long-term rise in inflation, and began to be reversed just as inflation was brought down in the early 1980s. The coefficients on lagged inflation in the U.S. manufacturing sector, therefore, may be picking up some of this change in relative wages and not be reflecting future manufacturing wage behavior. The coefficients on prior price changes are increased in the United States, the United Kingdom, and Italy if the dummy variables are removed. But the response of nominal wages to price changes is still larger in U.S. manufacturing than in other countries, except the United Kingdom.

---

which cover the period of the Nixon wage and price controls and the subsequent snapback, were excluded from the regression.

15. Gordon, "Wage-Price Dynamics."

Table 2-3. *Coefficients in Equations Explaining Wage Inflation in Manufacturing Industries, Five Countries, 1964–83*

Independent variable[a]	U.S. private nonfarm economy	Manufacturing				
		United States	United Kingdom	West Germany	Sweden	Italy
$\hat{q}$	0.25**	0.11	...	0.36**	0.36**	0.20
$\hat{Q}_{-1}$	0.23**	0.23**	0.78**	0.63**	0.69**	0.54**
p^v	0.63**	0.86**	0.41**	0.69**	0.49**	0.39**
$p^c - p^v$	0.67**	0.94**	0.84**	0.50**	0.13	0.14
$D_1{}^b$	2.12**	1.65	8.25**	6.57**	...	7.23**
Summary statistic						
$\bar{R}^2$	0.87	0.78	0.78	0.86	0.77	0.66
Standard error	0.70	1.22	3.22	1.22	1.76	3.77
Durbin-Watson	1.63	2.40	1.83	2.22	2.53	1.75

Source: Author's calculations.
** Significant at 5 percent level.

a. $\hat{q}$ = change in output relative to trend; $\hat{Q}$ = level of output relative to trend; p^v = rate of inflation in value-added prices; p^c = rate of inflation in the personal consumption deflator; and D_1 = norm shift dummy.

b. Norm shift dummies take on the value of 1.0 for years after 1968 for the United States and Italy and after 1970 for the United Kingdom; the German dummy takes on the value of 0.5 in 1969 and 1.0 in 1970 and zero in all other years. The period 1972–75 is excluded in the U.S. equation.

In the United States nominal wages responded to both components of price change by about the same amount. In the three Continental countries the immediate response of wages to price-raising supply shocks was less than the wage response to changes in value-added prices. Only in the United Kingdom was the response to supply-shock increases larger than the response to changes in domestic value-added prices. Gordon, using a weighted average of the results of equations for eleven European countries and the United States, also found that the response of nominal wage changes to price-raising supply shocks was much less in Europe than in the United States.[16]

The equations I used for the price-wage margin allow for a number of factors that, in principle, should influence the markup of prices relative to labor unit costs and therefore help determine the behavior

16. Ibid., table 6, p. 49. For a weighted average of Europe as a whole, his coefficient ($p^c - p^v$) variable is a low 0.30. His estimates for many individual countries, however, differ significantly from mine.

of real wages. The extent of unused capacity—measured by the ratio of output to its trend—may influence gross markups. In a neoclassical interpretation marginal costs rise as the utilization of capacity increases, and the aggregate supply curve expressed in terms of the price-wage margin will therefore slope upward. An alternative explanation for the same behavior is that firms set prices by a markup over long-run average costs, but take some advantage of industry-wide capacity shortages to improve their markup and conversely shade their markup in periods of recession when there is ample unused capacity.

In a small country operating in competitive world markets, prices of tradable goods produced domestically would be set by the domestic currency value of international prices. In the large countries of Western Europe, and even more so in the United States, manufacturing firms, operating in an environment that is a mixture of competition and oligopoly, have some room to vary the prices they charge relative to international price levels. Changes in foreign prices will affect markups but will not control them absolutely, as domestic manufacturers, in a less than complete but still substantial way, compete for exports in world markets and against imports in home markets. And so to the extent that the domestic currency value of foreign tradable goods prices rises relative to domestic standard unit labor costs, domestic price markups will tend to rise, and vice versa. Finally, even after controlling for capacity utilization and exchange rates, the speed with which increases in unit labor costs are passed on into prices may vary from country to country depending on the structure of labor and product markets.

On the basis of these considerations, the specific margin equations I used assume that prices are marked up on standard unit labor costs but with a lag that is allowed to vary among countries. The markups are allowed to vary in response to two major sets of factors: first, demand and supply conditions as measured by the ratio of actual output to its trend; and second, the extent of foreign competition in tradable goods, as measured by the ratio of foreign manufactured goods prices (converted to domestic currency units) to domestic standard unit labor costs. The equations were fit in the following form (in levels of logs):

Table 2-4. *Regression Results for Price-Wage Margin Equations, Five Countries, 1964–83*[a]

Independent variable[b]	U.S. private nonfarm economy[b]	Manufacturing				
		United States[b]	United Kingdom	West Germany	Sweden	Italy
Σ SULC[c] 3	0.97**	0.87**	0.96**	1.03**	1.03**	1.05**
$SULC_0$[d]	0.31**	0.48**	0.55**	0.74**	0.73**	0.52**
$\hat{Q}_{-1}$[e]	0.57**	0.28**	-0.18	-1.10	-0.01	-0.04
Σ PFOR$_{-1}$[c] 3	0.12**	0.15*	0.11	0.31**	0.78**	0.61**
Summary statistic						
$\bar{R}^2$	1.000	0.998	0.999	0.997	0.997	0.999
Standard error	0.005	0.012	0.019	0.014	0.024	0.020
ρ	-0.098	-0.070	-0.126	-0.725	0.080	0.269

Source: Author's calculations.
* Significant at 10 percent level.
** Significant at 5 percent level.
a. Data in levels of logs. All equations corrected for autocorrelations of residuals (Orchutt-Cochrane).
b. U.S. equation included two dummy variables, 1972–73 and 1974–75, to take out the imposition and withdrawal of Nixon price controls.
c. $\Sigma SULC$ and $\Sigma PFOR_{-1}$ are the sums of the coefficients on the relevant variables in an
    3   3
unconstrained first-order Almon lag. In the case of the SULC variable the first term is contemporaneous with the dependent variable; the first term in the exchange rate variable $PFOR_{-1}$ is lagged one year.
d. Coefficient on first term in distributed lag.
e. In U.S. equations the coefficients shown for the variable $\hat{Q}_{-1}$ are the sum of coefficients in a three-period first-order unconstrained Almon lag of $\hat{Q}_{-1}$.

$$(2\text{-}2) \quad P_t^v = b_0 + b_1 (L)SULC_t + b_2(L)\hat{Q}_{-1} + b_3 (L)PFOR_{-1},$$

where

P^v = value-added prices

$SULC$ = standard unit labor costs

$\hat{Q}$ = ratio of output to trend

$PFOR$ = domestic currency value of foreign manufactured goods prices less domestic standard unit labor costs

(L) = first-order, three-term, unconstrained Almon lag operator.

The markup equations, when fit to the data for 1964 through 1983, turned up some expected and some surprising results (table 2-4). Not unexpectedly, the markup of prices over standard unit labor costs in the United States, while sensitive to the real exchange rate, was much less than in Germany, Sweden, and Italy. But after controlling for real exchange rates, I could find no significant responsiveness of European price-wage margins to economic slack, whereas in U.S. manufacturing and to a greater extent in the U.S. economy as a whole there was such an effect. (The effect took place gradually over a number of years but was nevertheless significant.) Moreover, after controlling for real exchange rates and economic slack, it appeared to take substantially longer to pass on unit labor cost increases in the United States than it did in Germany and Sweden, and a little longer than in the United Kingdom and Italy. The sum of the coefficients on unit labor costs was smaller for U.S. manufacturing than that of the other countries.[17]

In sum, manufacturing firms in Germany, Sweden, and Italy were sensitive in their markups to changes in the domestic currency value of another country's prices. But insofar as nominal exchange rates adjusted to keep real exchange rates constant, European firms were more prone than U.S. firms to mark prices up quickly on wage costs and to leave markups unchanged during economic slack.

Unlike the situation in the other three European countries, in the United Kingdom the real exchange rate had no significant effect on price-wage margins. This seems to confirm anecdotal evidence that U.K. manufacturing firms are not aggressive competitors either at home or in third markets.

I used the wage and margin equations (together with an ancillary coefficient from a regression equation that relates consumer prices to the real exchange rate variable used in equation 2-2) to simulate the effect on real wages and on inflation of various kinds of shocks for periods up to ten years. In these simulations I treated output and real exchange rates as exogenous, ignoring possible feedback effects from internal economic developments on those variables. I simulated four kinds of shocks: a price-raising supply shock measured by the change in consumer prices relative to value-added prices; a fall in output relative to its trend value; an exogenous wage increase; and changes in the real exchange rate.

---

17. If long lags are used for the output ratio in European countries, the sum of coefficients either has the "wrong" (negative) sign or is insignificant.

It is critical to specify the behavior of exchange rates in the simulations. In Sweden and Italy, and to a significant but lesser extent in Germany, movements in real exchange rates have a major effect on price-wage margins, and a lesser but still observable effect on wages through their effect on consumer prices (picked up by the $p^c - p^v$ term in the wage equation). On the one hand, there is little evidence to support the view that purchasing power parity holds in the short run, even in the absence of shifts in portfolio preferences. Nominal exchange rates do not adjust automatically to eliminate short-run changes in relative inflation rates. On the other hand, the effects of long-run exchange rates on price-wage margins are so strong in Sweden and Italy, and to a lesser extent in Germany, that simulations which do not adjust nominal exchange rates in response to demand or supply shocks begin to produce large effects on real wages after four or five years as real exchange rates get further and further out of line.

The simulations confirmed the widely held view that the response of inflation to changes in demand and supply conditions are more sluggish in the United States than in Europe. If nominal exchange rates adjust so as to keep real exchange rates constant (table 2-5), a 5 percent decline in the ratio of output to potential, sustained at that level for a couple of years, reduces the inflation rate in U.S. manufacturing by 1.2 percentage points. In Germany and Sweden the inflation rate falls by 3.6 percentage points; and in the United Kingdom and Italy it falls by about 2 percentage points.

For the first four years after a decline in the output ratio the level of real wages falls less in the United States than in all the European countries so long as nominal exchange rates adjust to keep real exchange rates stable. After the fourth year, however, U.S. manufacturing real wages continued to fall while they did not do so in the European countries, except in the United Kingdom.[18] A comparison

---

18. This long-term result, however, may be the result of a specification error in the equation. In all the European countries and in the U.S. private nonfarm economy as a whole, the sum of the coefficients on the wage equation is very close to 1.0. In the U.S. manufacturing industries the coefficients summed to 0.9. In the short and medium run this has had only a small effect on the simulation results; in the long run the cumulative effect becomes substantial.

Table 2-5. *Effects of a 5 Percent Change in the Output Gap in Five Countries If the Nominal Exchange Rate Adjusts*[a]
Percentage points

Year	U.S. private nonfarm economy	Manufacturing				
		United States	United Kingdom	West Germany	Sweden	Italy
		Change in real wage level				
1	0.9	0.3	0.0	0.5	0.5	0.5
2	0.8	0.5	1.7	0.9	0.9	1.5
4	-0.1	0.7	2.9	1.0	0.9	2.0
10	0.7	3.5	3.5	0.3	0.0	1.1
		Change in inflation rate				
1	0.4	0.3	0.0	1.3	1.3	0.5
2	1.4	1.2	2.1	3.6	3.6	1.9
4	3.3	2.7	4.9	6.8	6.0	3.7
10	2.8	3.5	6.2	10.2	7.1	4.7

Source: Author's calculations.
a. The nominal exchange rate is assumed to change so as to keep the real exchange rate constant. The simulations assume that the initial disturbance occurs only in the home country.

of tables 2-5 and 2-6 shows, however, that this response of real manufacturing wages to changes in demand and supply conditions depends importantly on the exchange rate assumptions one makes. If nominal exchange rates do not adjust upward or downward with the change in domestic inflation, the resulting change in the real exchange rate has a major effect on real wages in the European countries. Under these conditions an increase in the output ratio, generating domestic wage and price increases, leads to an appreciation in the real exchange rate that with a time lag puts substantial downward pressure on price-wage margins and leads to a large increase in real wages. Since exchange rate effects are much smaller in the United States than in Europe, U.S. real wages respond far less to changes in the output ratio than do European real wages.

Under conditions of unchanged real exchange rates, increases in aggregate demand are not associated with falling real wages in any country. If real wages for some reason do get out of line, the wage and margin equations suggest that a subsequent increase in aggregate demand will not reduce them but will raise them—temporarily in the three continental countries, permanently in the United States and the

Table 2-6. *Effects of a 5 Percent Change in the Output Gap in Five Countries If the Nominal Exchange Rate Does Not Adjust*[a]
Percentage points

Year	U.S. private nonfarm economy	Manufacturing				
		United States	United Kingdom	West Germany	Sweden	Italy
		Change in real wage level				
1	0.9	0.3	0.0	0.5	0.5	0.5
2	0.8	0.5	1.7	1.0	1.7	1.7
4	0.0	0.7	3.4	2.4	6.6	4.1
10	1.8	4.7	6.3	8.9	22.3	13.4
		Change in inflation rate				
1	0.4	0.3	0.0	1.3	1.3	0.5
2	1.4	1.2	2.1	3.4	2.8	1.6
4	3.0	2.6	4.2	5.0	1.6	2.0
10	2.0	2.0	4.7	3.9	1.0	1.4

Source: Author's calculations.
a. Since the nominal exchange rate does not adjust, the real exchange rate moves with changes in domestic unit labor costs. The simulations assume that the initial disturbance occurs only in the home country.

United Kingdom. This same result, of course, implies that output can and does expand cyclically without the accompaniment of falling real wages, so long as real exchange rates are not affected.

In Germany, Sweden, and Italy, an appreciation of real effective exchange rates puts a substantial squeeze on profit margins and raises real wages while lowering inflation (table 2-7). A one-time 5 percent appreciation in the exchange rate, subsequently maintained for four more years, would tend to raise real wages by 4 percentage points in Sweden, 3 percentage points in Italy, and 1½ percentage points in Germany. During the second, third, and fourth years, it would also lower the annual inflation rate by 1 to 2 percentage points in the three countries.

In Germany and Sweden, and to a smaller extent in Italy, real exchange rates appreciated and foreign competition increased significantly during part or all of the 1970s, and then fell in the early 1980s. In table 2-8 the inverse of the real exchange rate is shown as a decline in the price of foreign manufactured goods (expressed in home country currency units) relative to domestic unit labor costs. It was, in fact, this movement of real exchange rates that generated

Table 2-7. *Effects of a 5 Percent Appreciation in the Real Exchange Rate in Five Countries*[a]
Percentage points

Year	U.S. private nonfarm economy	Manufacturing				
		United States	United Kingdom	West Germany	Sweden	Italy
		Change in real wage level				
1	0.0	0.0	0.0	0.0	0.0	0.0
2	−0.1	−0.2	0.2	0.3	2.2	1.0
4	0.5	0.6	0.5	1.4	4.0	2.9
10	0.5	0.4	0.5	1.7	4.4	3.3
		Change in inflation rate				
1	0.0	0.0	0.0	0.0	0.0	0.0
2	−0.1	0.0	−0.4	−0.6	−2.2	−1.1
4	−0.5	−0.8	−0.2	−1.2	−1.5	−1.4
10	−0.1	−0.2	0.0	−0.2	−0.1	−0.1

Source: Author's calculations.
a. The assumed increase in the real exchange rate is a one-time phenomenon occurring in year 1. Thereafter the nominal exchange rate is assumed to move so as to prevent any further change in the real exchange rate. The simulations assume that the initial disturbance occurs only in the home country.

much of the change over the period in the real wage gap (relative to trend) within the three continental countries. Simple correlations of the cyclically adjusted wage gap on a distributed lag of the log of this foreign exchange variable, PFOR, gave the following results (t-statistics in parentheses):[19]

	West Germany	Sweden	Italy
Sum of coefficients on PFOR $(-1, -2, -3)$	−0.17	−0.42	−0.49
	(12.7)	(9.2)	(5.9)
$\bar{R}^2$	0.90	0.82	0.64
Standard error	0.011	0.015	0.023

Thus it was not real wage rigidities so much as movements in the real exchange rate that produced much of the rise in the wage gap during the 1970s. And it has been the decline in real exchange rates (the rise

19. The lag structure was the same as used in the price margin equations—a three-term unconstrained first-order Almon lag beginning in period $t - 1$. The PFOR variable is an inverse of the real exchange rate and hence carries a negative sign in the wage gap equation. The equations were fit to the period 1964–83.

Table 2-8. *Labor's Share of Income in Manufacturing and Foreign Prices Relative to Domestic Unit Labor Costs in West Germany, Sweden, and Italy, Selected Dates, 1964–83*[a]

Period or year	West Germany		Sweden		Italy	
	Labor's share of income	Relative foreign prices, lagged	Labor's share of income	Relative foreign prices, lagged	Labor's share of income	Relative foreign prices, lagged
1964–65	0.58	1.44	0.70	1.37	0.56	1.19
1969–71	0.58	1.41	0.75	1.26	0.59	1.13
1975–76	0.62	1.04	0.77	1.24	0.66	1.00
1978–80	0.65	0.95	0.79	1.08	0.62	1.00
1981	0.66	0.91	0.78	1.15	0.61	1.01
1982	0.64	0.94	0.75	1.16	0.59	1.01
1983	0.62	0.99	0.72	1.23	0.59	1.02

Source: Author's calculations.

a. Labor share adjusted to remove effects of cyclical changes in productivity. The relative foreign price variable is a three-term moving average of *LPFOR* lagged by one year.

in foreign prices relative to domestic unit costs) that largely helped correct the rise in the wage gap during the early 1980s.

If the simulation results can be relied on, the very large real exchange rate appreciation in Germany during the 1970s helps to explain two aspects of Germany's economic performance. First, the exchange rate appreciation greatly helped to moderate German domestic inflation. But, second, it caused a significant rise in the real wage rate relative to productivity, beyond the long-term changes warranted by the less than unitary elasticity of factor substitution in the production function. Some of the recent decline in real wages relative to productivity growth in Germany and other European countries is undoubtedly attributable to the fall in relative exchange rates over the last three to four years.

It is at least a reasonable hypothesis that large alterations in price-wage margins (and, therefore, in real wages) brought about by changes in real exchange rates do not have the same depressing effect on unemployment that is alleged to occur when the real wage changes come about for other reasons. If most firms producing tradable goods act as monopolistic competitors, a substantial appreciation in real exchange rates, and a consequent fall in the prices charged by foreign competitors, can be thought of as equivalent to an increase in the competitiveness of the market environment. Domestic producers will then be willing to produce and sell a given output at a lower price-wage margin.[20] The rise in real wages associated with this development will not directly lead to a rise in unemployment.

Under these circumstances one of the three connections between real wages and unemployment is broken—the labor-shedding phenomenon will be much weaker than alleged. It is still true, however, that the higher real wages may induce some extra substitution of capital for labor along long-run production function and may discourage investment in increased capacity, leading to at least a temporary increase in the level of unemployment at which inflationary pressure becomes a problem. In sum, the close association between real exchange rates and real wages in the three continental European countries suggests two conclusions at variance with the excess real wage hypothesis:

—An important part of the rise in real wages in some European countries was caused not so much by downward rigidity in wage-setting behavior but by changes in competitiveness generated by changes in real exchange rates;

—That part of the rise in real wages associated with movements in the real exchange rates is likely to have had less effect on employment than changes in real wages stemming from other sources.[21]

Autonomous Wage Increases

So long as nominal exchange rates are assumed to adjust in line with changes in domestic prices, the simulations show that real wages

20. Technically, the slope of the demand curves facing domestic producers of tradables becomes more elastic. The gap between price and marginal cost narrows. Thus, even if firms are operating on their notional labor demand curves, this particular fall in prices relative to wages will not directly induce lower employment.

21. The appreciation in real exchange rates, if not offset by other demand increases, may, of course, reduce aggregate demand, and if producers are operating off their notional labor demand curves, employment may fall. But what is relevant here is that to the extent producers do operate on their notional labor demand curves, an appreciation in real exchange rates raises those demand curves, so that at any given real wage firms will seek to produce more output and demand more labor.

Table 2-9. *Effects of a One-Time Autonomous 5 Percent Wage Increase in Five Countries If the Nominal Exchange Rate Adjusts*[a]
Percentage points

| Year | U.S. private nonfarm economy | Manufacturing | | | | |
		United States	United Kingdom	West Germany	Sweden	Italy
		Change in real wage level				
1	3.4	2.5	2.2	1.3	1.3	2.4
2	2.4	2.1	1.1	0.3	0.1	1.1
4	1.6	2.2	0.6	0.0	−0.1	0.1
10	0.6	2.2	0.3	−0.3	−0.3	−0.3
		Change in inflation rate				
1	1.5	2.4	2.8	3.7	3.6	2.6
2	1.9	2.4	2.2	3.6	3.0	2.3
4	1.2	1.7	0.7	1.9	1.0	0.8
10	0.3	0.6	0.0	0.4	0.0	0.0

Source: Author's calculations.
a. The nominal exchange rate is assumed to change so as to keep the real exchange rate constant. The simulations assume that the initial disturbance occurs only in the home country.

in Europe were less affected by an autonomous increase in nominal wages than they were in the United States (tables 2-9 and 2-10). Again, this result stems from the slower adjustment of prices to changes in unit labor costs in the United States, given stability in demand conditions and real exchange rates. In the late 1960s Europe did have an autonomous wage explosion that had some effect on real wages—and a much larger effect on inflation. The United States did not have such a wage explosion, but if there had been one, the effect on real wages would have been more severe and lasted longer than in Europe.

Contrary to accepted wisdom, it is in the United States where supply shocks have the largest effect on both product real wages and inflation, so long as it is assumed that the nominal exchange rates adjust to keep the real exchange rate constant (table 2-11). Moreover, the increase in product real wages persists in U.S. manufacturing industries, whereas it disappears after four or five years in the three Continental countries and declines sharply in the United Kingdom. The large lag in passing through induced wage increases into prices and the less-than-unitary sum of coefficients of prices in unit labor

Table 2-10. *Effects of a One-Time Autonomous 5 Percent Wage Increase in Five Countries If the Nominal Exchange Rate Does Not Adjust*[a]

Percentage points

Year	U.S. private nonfarm economy	Manufacturing			Sweden	Italy
		United States	United Kingdom	West Germany		
		Change in real wage level				
1	3.4	2.5	2.2	1.3	1.3	2.4
2	2.3	1.9	1.3	0.6	2.2	2.1
4	2.0	2.7	1.1	1.8	4.8	3.2
10	1.5	3.1	1.0	2.4	4.1	3.2
		Change in inflation rate				
1	1.5	2.4	2.8	3.7	3.6	2.6
2	1.8	2.5	1.8	3.0	0.8	1.2
4	0.6	0.8	0.3	0.1	−1.5	−0.9
10	0.1	0.0	0.0	0.0	0.0	0.0

Source: Author's calculations.

a. Since the nominal exchange rate does not adjust, the real exchange rate moves with changes in domestic unit labor costs. The simulations assume that the initial disturbance occurs only in the home country.

costs exert a relatively large upward force on U.S. manufacturing real wages when supply shocks occur. Moreover, since margins in the United States, but not in Europe, are sensitive to increases in economic slack, any tendency for supply shocks to reduce output would widen the difference between the response of real wages in the United States and that in Europe.

I think several important conclusions about the contrast between European and U.S. wage and price behavior can be drawn from this analysis of the determinants of real and nominal wages. First, the factors that determine real wages are many and complex; one cannot say that real wages are or are not rigid except in the context of a number of conditions. In the same country real wages may be rigid in response to some shocks and flexible in response to others. Second, it is not correct to say that Europe suffers from real wage rigidity while the United States is afflicted with nominal wage rigidity. My analysis of manufacturing industries shows that nominal wages and the inflation rate in U.S. manufacturing industries do indeed respond more sluggishly to changes in demand conditions than they do in

Table 2-11. *Effects of a 5 Percent Supply Shock If the Nominal Exchange Rate Adjusts*[a]
Percentage points

Year	U.S. private nonfarm economy	Manufacturing				
		United States	United Kingdom	West Germany	Sweden	Italy
		Change in real wage level				
1	0.0	0.0	0.0	0.0	0.0	0.0
2	2.3	2.4	1.8	0.6	0.2	0.3
4	0.9	2.0	0.6	0.2	0.0	0.0
10	0.5	2.1	0.3	−0.1	0.0	−0.1
		Change in inflation rate				
1	0.0	0.0	0.0	0.0	0.0	0.0
2	1.0	2.3	2.3	1.9	0.5	0.4
4	1.6	2.0	1.1	1.2	0.2	0.2
10	0.3	0.6	0.0	0.2	0.0	0.0

Source: Author's calculations.

a. A supply shock, as here defined, raises the level of the difference between consumer prices and domestic manufacturing value-added prices ($p^c - p^v$) by 5 percent.

Europe. And another analysis, which I have reported on elsewhere, suggests that the same contrast between the United States and Europe holds up when entire economies (and not just their manufacturing sectors) are compared.[22] But so long as one controls for real exchange rates, real product wages are also less flexible in the United States than in Europe; that is, they are more prone to rise relative to their warranted level in responding to supply shocks or autonomous nominal wage increases, and more sluggish in responding to restrictive demand management. In the three continental European countries, however, the level of price-cost margins, and hence the level of real wages, is far more sensitive to the real exchange rate than it is in the United States. From the late 1960s until 1980, the period of worldwide supply shocks and the European wage explosion, the real exchange rate of each of the three continental European countries appreciated. In the United States it fell. It was this development, I suspect, that was the main reason for different patterns of real wage behavior. Finally, there

22. Charles L. Schultze, "Cross-Country and Cross-Temporal Differences in Inflation Responsiveness," *American Economic Review*, vol. 74 (May 1984, *Papers and Proceedings, 1983*), pp. 160–65.

is at least a plausible reason to believe that changes in real wages stemming from alterations in real exchange rates may have less effect on employment, especially in the short run, than is assumed in the usual exposition of the European real wage hypothesis.

A major shortcoming of my analysis is that real exchange rates are treated as an exogenous variable. To the extent nominal exchange rates adjust to the price changes that result from the various economic shocks I have simulated, so as to keep real exchange rates constant, the conclusions I have reached are legitimate: wages in Europe are not more rigid than those in the United States in response to supply shocks. But if in any of the three continental countries there is some mechanism that systematically and substantially appreciates real exchange rates when a worldwide supply shock occurs, real wages in that country will in fact perform more rigidly than in the United States. If during the 1970s, for example, market participants believed that Germany would do a better job of containing inflation than others when unfavorable worldwide supply shocks occurred, that belief may have been partly self-justifying. That is, the resultant appreciation in the exchange rate may have helped contain inflation, though at the expense of an excessive rise in German real wages and a squeeze on profits. According to conventional analysis, stimulative fiscal (IS) shocks combined with a nonaccommodative monetary policy tend to appreciate the real exchange rate while stimulative monetary shocks depreciate it. Thus the effect of demand shocks on real wages will depend on their source.

Microeconomic Sources of Differences in Behavior: Some Speculation

Several of the differences between the United States and Europe in the behavior of wages and margins that have emerged from the equations and simulations seem, at least on the surface, to be explainable by some institutional and structural characteristics of the countries involved. The wage equations suggest that changes in manufacturing unit labor cost are passed into prices more quickly in Germany and Sweden than they are in the United States, once one controls for real exchange rates and demand conditions. This apparent difference is, I think, explainable by the much more fragmented, decentralized, and time-staggered nature of wage setting in the United States. In Germany and Sweden wage bargains tend to be more centralized and clustered around a central time period. Insofar as nominal exchange rates can be expected to adjust to reflect differences in inflation rates, firms in those countries are somewhat more able than firms in the United States to project their own wage increases into the costs of other firms that directly or indirectly compete with them. The more sluggish pass-through of wage costs in the United States is not inconsistent with the nature of wage bargaining here.

That price markups over unit labor costs are more sensitive to the state of demand in the United States suggests—not unreasonably— that there is more competitiveness among U.S. business firms within the country than among firms within each of the European countries. Conversely, the larger effect on European price-wage margins of movements in the real exchange rate implies that foreign competition provides a more important source of discipline over prices in Europe than in the United States.

Finally, the simulations indicate that a large autonomous wage increase in the United States would have a bigger effect in squeezing profit margins than it would in Europe. It may, then, be no coincidence that the United States in the postwar period seems to have had no exogenous wage explosions to compare with the widely documented one that occurred in Europe in the late 1960s.

Conclusion

In this lecture I have sought to show that real wages in Europe are neither as excessive nor as downwardly rigid as is commonly believed. By 1983 the widely used measure of excess real wages—the rise in labor's share of value added, or what is the same thing, the growth in real product wages relative to productivity—was larger in Japan and the United States than in Europe. Moreover, the rise in European real product wages relative to productivity began more than twenty-five years ago, and part of it was a natural and nonthreatening consequence of Europe's rapid postwar growth.

Just as the size of the excess in European real wages has been exaggerated, so has their downward rigidity. Increases in real exchange rates do tend to raise real wages in Europe substantially and by much more than is true in the United States. But if real exchange rates are stable, real product wages in European manufacturing increase less in response to outside supply shocks and to exogenous nominal wage increases, and yield more readily to restrictive demand policies, than they do in U.S. manufacturing. The widely accepted view that U.S. real wages are more flexible than European real wages in response to supply disturbances is not borne out by the empirical evidence from fitting wage and price equations to the data of the past twenty years.

The results of this analysis do not imply that the level of wages in European countries is in some sense optimal. Nor do they deal in any comprehensive way with the question of the extent to which changes in real wages affect output and employment decisions. But they strongly argue that it is unwarranted to identify downwardly rigid real wages as the chief culprit in Europe's poor economic performance.

Notes on Data Sources

For European countries the $\hat{Q}$ variable in equations 2-1 and 2-2 is the deviation of manufacturing output from a trend, constructed as a centered nine-term moving average of manufacturing output extrapolated from 1977 to 1983 with the 1976 trend.[23] For the United States private nonfarm sector, trend output was constructed by subtracting government output and an estimate of trend farm output from Robert Gordon's estimates of potential GNP (*BPEA, 2:1984*, appendix A-1, p. 563). Trend output in U.S. manufacturing was estimated from a time trend on output, 1950–79 (with a trend shift in 1973), extrapolated through 1983.

23. For Italy the mean of the 1975 and 1976 rate of change in the nine-term average was extrapolated. For the United Kingdom the rate of change in the centered nine-term average was less than $\frac{1}{2}$ percent a year for 1976 and 1977 and the level of trend output was held constant from 1977 on.

The data on manufacturing compensation per hour, productivity, and value-added prices for all countries were taken from estimates regularly published by the U.S. Bureau of Labor Statistics. The real exchange rate data from which the PFOR variable in equation 2-2 was derived is the International Monetary Fund's series on relative value-added deflators ("Cost and Price Comparisons for Manufacturing," series 99by 110, in *International Financial Statistics*). That variable was divided by the BLS manufacturing value-added deflator and inverted to produce an index of the price of foreign manufactured goods in home-country currency units.

III

A Century of U.S. Economic Fluctuations: Why Has Performance Improved?

This final lecture is essentially an externality spun off from the examination of early twentieth-century data that provided the material for my first lecture. A long-recognized feature of the statistical record is that economic instability in the United States during the seventy years before the Second World War was much greater than it has been in the last four decades. This conclusion is still true even when the years of the Great Depression and the exceedingly sharp downturn of 1919–21 are removed from the data. In fact, in the analysis presented here I exclude the years after 1914 from the earlier period.

In the first lecture I gave some comparisons between the pre-1914 and the post–World War II periods. Let me repeat them quickly and flesh them out some more. For convenience I call the years before 1914 the prewar years and those since World War II the postwar years. According to the National Bureau of Economic Research (NBER) monthly chronology, during the forty-four years from 1871 through 1914 the U.S. economy spent half of the time in expansion and half in contraction. From 1945 through 1983 the ratio of expansion time to contraction time was in the very different ratio of 4 to 1. The amplitude of the prewar cycles was also much larger. The standard deviation of annual changes in GNP relative to trend growth was more than twice as great from 1871 through 1914 as it was between 1953 and 1983. And the two parts of the prewar period,

59

1871–90 and 1891–1914, were about equally unstable. In the two largest contractions of the postwar years the decline in real GNP, measured on an annual basis, averaged 2 percent. In the forty-four years from 1871 through 1914 there were six large contractions averaging more than 4 percent. The two periods also differed in the shape of their business cycles. The mean length of expansion in the prewar period was twenty-five months, only slightly longer than the twenty-three-month mean length of contractions. Postwar contractions lasted, on average, only half as long as their early predecessors, whereas expansions were almost twice the length. As I noted in the first lecture, the prewar cycle, measured around trend, usually took the form of a deep symmetrical V, while the postwar cycles usually took the form of a shallow check mark, with the right hand stroke much longer than the left.

This contrast between prewar and postwar cycles is especially characteristic of the United States. From 1954 through 1983 the standard deviation of percent changes in GNP in five major countries (the United States, the United Kingdom, West Germany, Sweden, and Italy) fell within a narrow range, from 2.0 to 2.3 percentage points. From 1871 through 1914, the range of standard deviation among the countries was very much greater. The United States' deviation was significantly larger than those of the others, at 5.9 percentage points. At the other extreme the variance in output in the United Kingdom was virtually the same during the two periods, with other countries falling in between. If the numbers can be believed, the very large size of prewar economic fluctuations in the United States was not a universally shared characteristic.

Do the Early Data Overstate Economic Instability?

A recent series of papers by Christina Romer has challenged the validity of the annual Kuznets, Lebergott, and derivative data for those early years.[1] In particular, Romer argues that the interpolating

1. See Christina Romer, "New Estimates of Unemployment and Gross National Product for the U.S.: A 96-Year History" (and references to other papers cited therein), paper presented at the 1985 meeting of the Economic History Association, New York City, September 20, 1985.

techniques used by Kuznets and Lebergott to estimate annual data between the years of the census and other benchmark series substantially overstated the volatility of the prewar economy. She particularly criticizes Lebergott's use of commodity flow data to interpolate employment in the trade and service industries. When the numbers are corrected to remove what she believes to be systematic errors exaggerating their annual variance, Romer concludes that the magnitude of pre–World War II business cycles, outside the Great Depression, was much less than commonly believed, and not much larger than the variance in the postwar economy.

David Weir has undertaken a detailed analysis of the Romer articles.[2] In regard to the employment and unemployment data, he has painstakingly reconstructed an annual series himself, using alternative data and estimating techniques when he finds the Lebergott approach wanting. He concludes that although the volatility of the prewar estimates may be somewhat exaggerated in Kuznets and Lebergott, the degree of overstatement is far less than Romer claims. The variance in output and unemployment in the prewar period is still very much larger than that in the postwar years. I agree with Weir's conclusions and will add only a few additional points to support his findings.

In the first place, comparisons of the volatility of various macroeconomic data as between prewar and postwar years all point in the same direction. The table below gives, for eight macroeconomic variables, the ratios of the prewar (1891–1914) to the postwar standard deviation of annual percent change in those variables:

Variable	Ratio
Real GNP	2.1
Nominal GNP	2.2
Business fixed investment	2.4
Civilian employment	2.3
Nonfarm aggregate hours worked (Kendrick)	1.7
Manufacturing production	1.8
Steel production	1.8
Money supply	1.7

2. David Weir, "Okun's Law and the Curious Stability of Historical Unemployment Estimates," paper presented at the 1985 meeting of the Economic History Association, New York City, September 20, 1985.

There are some dependent relationships among several of the series: Lebergott, for example, used output measures to interpolate some of his employment series. But he had a surprisingly large number of censuses and sample employment surveys to work with, and his estimates of employment have a large—though not complete—degree of independence from the output data. The smaller ratio of prewar to postwar standard deviations for the last four series—nonfarm aggregate hours, industrial production, steel output, and money supply—might argue that the prewar volatility was a little less than twice as great rather than a little more than twice as great as postwar volatility. But the difference in the stability of the two periods is still very large.

I fit a cyclical productivity equation for the private nonfarm economy to the two periods, by using Kendrick's series on aggregate hours of labor input for the prewar years.[3] Though some of his industry employment series were interpolated annually by output data, Kendrick tells us that most of them were independently derived. The productivity equation had the same form as the one described in my second lecture. Essentially it related cyclical deviations in productivity around their trend path to both the rate of change and the trend-adjusted level of output. The coefficient on the change in output was quite similar in both periods. But the equation showed that the level of output had a positive effect on productivity growth in the prewar period and no significant effect in the postwar years. Conceivably the prewar effect could have been produced by erroneous measures of output that showed excessive cyclical fluctuations. And so I proportionately compressed the annual distribution of prewar output around its trend by a sufficient amount to force the prewar and postwar productivity equations to tell approximately the same story. The standard deviation of annual percent change in the resulting prewar output series was still 1.9 times its postwar level. This fits with the earlier suggestion that the volatility of prewar output may have been a little less than twice as great as it was in the postwar period—still a very substantial difference.

3. John W. Kendrick, *Productivity Trends in the United States*, National Bureau of Economic Research series 71 (Princeton University Press, 1961), p. 311.

Finally, one of the elements in Romer's critique of the prewar data is the assumption that the relative structure of employment and output variance was the same in the prewar and postwar periods. Thus she replicates for the postwar period what she interprets to be Lebergott's annual estimators for employment, finds that they overstate the actual postwar variance, and assumes that they therefore overstate the prewar variance. By this reasoning, Lebergott's technique would have especially overstated the variance in trade and service employment. Some of the later analysis in this lecture, however, strongly suggests that the structure of the cyclical variance in employment and output changed significantly between the prewar and postwar periods. In particular, the variance in output and employment in consumer-goods industries, and hence in trade and services, may have been much greater relative to the variance in commodity output than is now true. And so any bias that did arise from excessive use by Lebergott and Kuznets of commodity-flow interpolations is likely to be smaller than what can be inferred from the postwar relationship of trade and services to the rest of the economy.

Without pretending to a detailed knowledge of the construction of the prewar data, I judge from reviewing the evidence that the income, output, and employment series may indeed exaggerate the cyclical variance of the prewar economy, but that even after correction the remaining cyclical volatility was still much greater than it has been for the past three or four decades.

Money Supply and Interest Rates in Prewar Business Cycles

The instability of the nineteenth-century economy is often attributed to the exogenous instability of the money supply combined with the rigid upper limits to that supply imposed by the gold standard. An erratic supply of money generated erratic swings in income and spending. Under the operation of the international gold standard, domestic expansion led to an outflow of gold, which in turn suddenly braked the expansion and threw the economy into decline. A related and not inconsistent variation attributes some part of the instability to the imperfections of an unregulated, fractional reserve banking system without the presence of a central bank. After a period of strong loan expansion the American banking system often generated liquidity crises and financial panics that dried up the source of financing for real economic activity. I believe, however, that there is some highly suggestive, even if not conclusive, evidence that the prewar cycles were dominated by a different process along Wicksellian lines.[4] Far from being exogenous, the money supply was highly endogenous: it was very responsive to changes in income, generated by the combination of volatile investment demand and a relatively large Keynesian multiplier.[5] This process can be heuristically depicted as one in which large variations in the IS curve impinged on an elastic LM curve, whose flatness derived not from a highly interest elastic demand for money but from the endogeneity of the money supply, responding positively to changes in the demand for money.

If the driving mechanism of the nineteenth and early twentieth centuries business cycles had been an exogenous and highly variable money supply, one should find large increases in interest rates preceding upper turning points in the cycle and large decreases at cycle troughs. And if this process had been accompanied in the later stages of expansion by financial disintermediation, brought on by liquidity crises in the banking system, there is more reason to have expected a sharp peaking up of interest rates before cycle turning points. Heuristically again, this version of the prewar cyclical process can be pictured as a volatile LM curve shifting up and down a relatively stable IS curve. In the financial panic version, much of the action would be concentrated near the upper turning points.

As I have presented them, the critical difference between these two contradictory views of the mechanism underlying the prewar business cycle is in what they predict about the cyclical behavior of interest rates. But before looking at the evidence with respect to interest rates,

4. Knut Wicksell attributed the expansion phases of business cycles to the combination of expanding investment demand and the operation of the commercial banking system, which readily expanded credit to meet the demand for it at relatively constant interest rates. Thus the "market" rate of interest was held below the "natural" rate.

5. As suggested below, consumers then had little access to consumer credit or to liquid reserves and hence their consumption was closely dependent on current disposable income.

I need to consider several possible objections to the use of interest rate behavior as a means of discriminating between the two views.

First, if prices were highly flexible and moved quickly to clear markets, changes in the money supply would not, even in the short run, be inversely related to nominal interest rates. But as I discussed in the first lecture, the short-run response of the final prices of goods to changes in nominal demand shocks was no less sticky in the prewar period than in the postwar period. And in any event, if prices had rapidly moved to clear markets, we would not be sitting here asking why the volatility of output was so great during those years.

Second, what about the possibility that exogenous changes in the money supply found their way directly into the hands of consumers and spilled over into changes in the demand for goods and services without passing through the market for loanable funds? If so, large exogenous swings in the money supply could have shifted both the IS and LM curves in the same direction, generating the prewar business cycles without the effects on interest rates that I postulated earlier.

Friedman and Schwartz, in the third volume of their trilogy on money, while recognizing that the short-run effect of an increase in the money supply (M2) can reduce interest rates, suggest two possible ways in which increases in the money supply may pass directly into the hands of consumers and, without any fall in interest rates, produce an increased demand for goods.[6] In the first way the monetary change would take the form of increases in gold production: the income of gold miners and mine operators would rise and their demand for goods and services would change accordingly. In the second way newly issued money would go directly into the hands of government and be associated with increases in government spending. Another possible way for additional M2 to enter directly into spending is through exogenous shocks to the foreign trade sector, leading to a change in the trade balance financed by net imports of gold. Changes in that component of M2 would be directly associated with changes in income.

However interesting these are as possibilities, they do not describe

6. Milton Friedman and Anna J. Schwartz, *Monetary Trends in the United States and the United Kingdom: Their Relation to Income, Prices, and Interest Rates, 1867–1975* (University of Chicago Press, 1982), pp. 483–84.

monetary changes in the period that I am investigating. For one thing, in a simple regression only 4 percent of the annual absolute changes in M2 can be accounted for by simultaneous changes in gold stocks (and only 22 percent when gold stocks are lagged one year). And in any event, 77 percent of the variance of annual changes in the gold supply itself can be accounted for by net imports of gold. Thus, in the short run, changes in domestic gold production were not the main source of annual changes in gold stocks, which in turn were not closely associated with cyclical changes in the money supply.

The proposition that changes in the money supply were generated to finance the federal budget deficit also has no foundation in the data. Federal deficits and surpluses in the early years were far too small to explain changes in the money supply. The standard deviation of the federal deficit was only one-seventh as large as the standard deviation of the money supply, and there is no correlation between the two series.

Net gold imports were not a route by which changes in the money supply went directly into the hands of consumers or investors. The correlation between the absolute value of annual changes in M2 and net gold imports, while positive, is statistically indistinguishable from zero in the prewar years. And the standard deviation of net gold imports is only one-sixteenth the size of the standard deviation of annual absolute changes in the money supply. Changes in the money supply therefore took none of the routes by which they could have directly affected the market for goods while bypassing the market for loanable funds.

Because of the short-run stickiness of final-goods prices in the prewar years, which both Robert Gordon and I have investigated,[7] and the absence of a direct connection between changes in the money supply and the market for goods, the behavior of interest rates relative to that of other economic variables can indeed help to discriminate between the two alternative interpretations of the cyclical behavior of the money supply during the period.

7. Robert J. Gordon, "A Consistent Characterization of a Near Century of Price Behavior," *American Economic Review*, vol. 70 (May 1980, *Papers and Proceedings, 1979*), pp. 243–49; and Charles L. Schultze, "Some Macro Foundations for Micro Theory," *Brookings Papers on Economic Activity, 2:1981*, pp. 521–76.

The Behavior of Interest Rates

On the basis of annual data, during the business cycles of 1891–1914 the average increase in commercial paper rates in the last two years of cyclical expansions was 0.1 percentage point. In sharp contrast, increases in commercial paper rates averaged 1.7 percentage points in the last two years of postwar expansions (excluding the period after the change in the Federal Reserve's regime in 1979, when, of course, the increases were even larger).[8] The fall in short-term rates during contractions averaged 0.8 percentage points in prewar recessions but double that amount, 1.7 percentage points, in postwar recessions.

Similarly, the standard deviation of annual changes in short-term commercial paper rates in the prewar period was either the same as or somewhat less than that in the postwar years (depending on which of two alternative time series is used), even though the standard deviation in both nominal and real GNP was more than twice as large in the prewar period.[9] During 1953–83 the ratio of the standard deviation of changes in short-term interest rates to the standard deviation of changes in both real and nominal GNP was about two and one-half times as large as it was in 1871–1914. A similar relationship holds when the subperiod 1891–1914 is compared with the postwar period. The ratio approaches 3 to 1 in the earlier subperiod 1871–90. As for long-term bond rates, the prewar volatility was very small. Indeed, the standard deviation of annual changes in Macaulay's railroad bond yields over the whole forty-four year period was an incredibly low twenty-four basis points. When changes in short-term

8. In the analysis of interest rates that follows, I exclude the years after 1979, when the Federal Reserve's operating regime was changed. Had those years been included, the postwar volatility of interest rates would appear even larger, relative to the prewar situation, than my discussion suggests.

9. One series is published by the Federal Reserve, and for 1890–1910 uses estimates produced by W. C. Mitchell. This is series 445 in U.S. Bureau of the Census, *Historical Statistics of the United States: Colonial Times to 1970* (Government Printing Office, 1975), pt. 2, p. 1001. The other series, which has somewhat more annual variance, is the one published by Frederick R. Macaulay and reproduced in Friedman and Schwartz, *Monetary Trends*, table 4.8, pp. 122–26.

interest rates are correlated with current and lagged changes in real GNP, the sum of the coefficients is 0.23 in the prewar period (1871–1914) and 0.59 in the postwar years (1953–78).

One cannot offer the explanation that capital markets were imperfect during the prewar period, that quantity rationing of bank loans was the rule, and that interest rates are not a good indicator of the pressures of excess demand or supply on the credit markets. The short-term interest rates I have been using are commercial paper rates, that is, open market rates. Even if—indeed especially if—quantity rationing by banks were the rule, a period of very restrictive rationing should be accompanied by large changes in open market rates, which were the alternative source of funding for large established borrowers.

This comparison of cyclical interest rate movements does not conform with the predictions of any model that attributes the prewar cyclical instability to an exogenously shifting money supply—interest rate variance should have been much larger. The evidence in favor of the financial panic explanation is not better. In an early history of the period O. W. M. Sprague identified a number of financial panics.[10] Using Robert Gordon's estimates of quarterly GNP from 1892 to 1910, Delong and Summers calculated standard deviations of the changes in output and in the level of output relative to potential output for that period, first as a whole and then with the three quarters and the seven quarters surrounding "financial panics" removed.[11] The size of the standard deviation of output change, or of the output gap, was not significantly affected by removing the periods around panics.

A simple inspection of monthly interest rates around NBER cyclical turning points or around Sprague panic dates is enough to cast grave doubt on the panic thesis, and to bolster the evidence for the

10. O. W. M. Sprague, *History of Crises under the National Banking Act* (GPO, 1910).

11. Delong and Summers used alternative definitions of financial panics: one included the panics identified by Sprague and the other employed their own classifications based on those times when short-term interest rates jumped by more than 1 percentage point in a month. Ibid., pp. 17–23. Despite my disagreement with Delong and Summers on their interpretation of the evidence on price flexibility, their paper was the inspiration for much of what follows here. J. Bradford Delong and Lawrence Summers, "The Changing Cyclical Variability of Economic Activity in the United States," Discussion Paper 1077 (Harvard University, Institute of Economic Research, August 1984).

endogeneity of the money supply. Interest rates in overnight money (call rates) did shoot up for several months around many of the panic dates. But short-term commercial paper rates did so much less frequently, and when they did, the peak typically did not last more than two to four months. Long-term bond rates were virtually unchanged.

A more careful examination of the behavior of interest rates around NBER monthly turning points is instructive. Between 1890 and 1914 there were eight business-cycle peaks, three of which were associated with so-called financial panics. On only one of those eight occasions— the panic and turning point in the summer of 1893—did commercial paper rates move up sharply and stay there for a long time. After the upper turning point in five of the remaining seven cycles, commercial paper rates rose modestly, by 1.2 to 1.4 percentage points, for three to four months and then receded; in the other two cycles rates did not move up at all.

Moreover, in only two of the eight cycles did short-term interest rates move up significantly in the six months before the peak. Given any reasonable lag structure, this fact is hard to square with the view that stringency in the money supply was the driving force in the cycle. Moreover, in no recession did it take less than ten months for short-term interest rates to fall below their level at the upper turning point, and in six of the eight cycles it took twelve months or more for rates to fall below that level. This is fully consistent with the existence of a money supply function under which money supplies contracted as the demand for money fell. The frequent occurrence of modest and short-lived interest rate increases after the NBER peaks suggests that downturns may have produced some disintermediation and liquidity squeezes. But the liquidity squeezes appeared to be the product of the cycle rather than the cause.

I believe that several important phenomena were at work in the early period. The first was the existence of a banking system that generated an endogenous money supply, highly elastic to changes in national income. The standard deviation of the money supply (Friedman-Schwartz M2) around a middle-expansion path was 4.3 percentage points in the early years 1891–1914 versus 1.6 percentage points in the postwar years. A middle expansion path is the course traced out by a variable between its values at the middle of each cyclical expansion. But, as noted above, if the early years were characterized by wide swings in an exogenously determined money supply—large fluctuations in an LM curve around a relatively stable IS curve—there should have been larger fluctuations in interest rates in the early years than in the postwar years. The opposite was true. The relative instability of nominal and real GNP can be made consistent with the relative stability of interest rates only if the swings in the money supply were highly endogenous—that is, large swings in an IS curve around an LM curve made highly elastic by an endogenously responding money supply. Conceivably, the observed facts of the early years—relative stability of interest rates combined with relative instability of GNP—could have been consistent with large exogenous swings in the money supply if aggregate demand had been much more sensitive to changes in the interest rates than in the postwar years. But there is no reason to believe that was true. In a recent paper Gordon and Veitch found that investment by business (and households) was much less sensitive to changes in the cost of capital in the interwar period, 1921–41, than in the years since the Second World War.[12] Though their analysis did not cover the pre-1914 period with which I am concerned here, their findings about the interwar period do establish a strong presumption that the investment demand curve in the early years was not more interest elastic than it has been in the postwar period.

The interpretation that the money supply was endogenous is consistent with the data in another way. If the money supply was itself a positive function of cyclical changes in income during the prewar period, this fact would tend to bias upward the interest elasticity of the LM curve derived from a demand-for-money function fitted to the period. And when a standard demand-for-money function is estimated for the prewar and postwar periods—distinguishing

12. Robert J. Gordon and John M. Veitch, "Fixed Investment in the American Business Cycle, 1919–83," National Bureau of Economic Research Working Paper 1426 (Cambridge, Mass.: NBER, August 1984). The coefficients on the user cost of capital (for business investment) and the real interest rate (for household investment) either had the wrong sign or were insignificant for the interwar years, but were positive and usually significant for the postwar years.

between cyclical and longer-term changes in money demand—the interest elasticity of the LM curve thereby revealed is from almost one and a half times to more than two times as large in the prewar as in the postwar years.[13] This evidence is not itself conclusive. The higher interest elasticity of the LM curve in the prewar period might have been generated by a genuinely larger negative interest elasticity of the underlying demand-for-money function. Since one cannot separately identify the money supply function, this remains a possibility. Nevertheless, a number of pieces of evidence point in the same direction: the size of the variance in interest rates relative to the variance in output and income; the simple regression of changes in interest rates on changes in output; the pattern of monthly interest rates before and after cyclical turning points; and the high cyclical interest elasticity of the LM curve. And that direction is the existence of an endogenous and procyclical money supply in the prewar years.

The endogeneity of the money supply in the early years was partly due to the ability of the banking system to generate additional money supplies independently of cash holdings. M2 varied substantially in relation to the quantity of high-powered money.[14] The reason for this lay principally in the behavior of commercial bank deposits relative to bank reserves. In the early years 96 percent of absolute changes in the money supply were typically composed of changes in bank deposits and only 4 percent of changes in currency.[15] In turn, expressing the data in logs, 57 percent of the changes in bank deposits were typically accounted for by changes in the deposit-to-reserve ratio and only 43 percent with changes in the quantity of bank reserves.[16] There was only a very low correlation between changes in deposits and changes

13. See appendix A. The Federal Reserve-Mitchell series on short-term interest rates generates a higher interest elasticity than the Macaulay series.

14. High-powered money in the prewar era was the sum of the currency held by the public and bank-vault cash. In the postwar years vault cash becomes very small, but member bank deposits and nonmember clearing accounts at the Federal Reserve are added.

15. Since the change in the money supply is the sum of changes in currency and changes in bank deposits, the simple regression coefficients of changes in currency on changes in money supply (0.04) and changes in bank deposits on changes in the money supply (0.96) add to 1.0. See appendix B.

16. In logs, the change in bank deposits is equal to the change in the quantity of reserves plus the change in the deposit-to-reserve ratio.

in reserves ($\bar{R}^2 = 0.10$). In the postwar years 1961–79, by contrast, changes in adjusted member bank reserves typically accounted for 91 percent of the change in commercial bank deposits and changes in the deposit-to-reserve ratio for only 9 percent.[17] There was a substantial correlation between changes in deposits and changes in reserves ($\bar{R}^2 = 0.67$). In the nineteenth and early twentieth centuries the banking system had far more flexibility than it now has to create credit freely in response to changes in the demand for money and so to generate a procyclical money supply function. The banking system thus operated along the lines of the "real bills" doctrine.

Some of the greater stability of output and employment in the postwar period occurred in part, I believe, because the managed money supply of the postwar years was less accommodative than it had been in the earlier period, with its supposedly rigid gold standard. The postwar money supply expanded less easily during booms and fell less freely during contractions. This behavior, in turn, generated relatively greater procyclical swings in interest rates, which helped stabilize the economy. What the Federal Reserve has done in the postwar period is to destroy much of the endogenous, procyclical nature of changes in the money supply, partly by creating a monetary system in which bank deposits are closely tied to bank reserves. It was largely the independence of deposits from reserves that made the prewar monetary system procyclical.

Though this analysis shows that the managed money of the postwar years was far less procyclical than money had been in the prewar period, it does not show whether money was on balance managed so as to be positively countercyclical. There were occasions—the submerged business cycle peak in 1959–60 is one of them—in which excessive caution by the Federal Reserve prematurely choked off recovery. The recession of 1982 was deliberately incurred as a means of wringing out inflation. In 1972, and possibly in 1978–79, one might argue that the Fed was too accommodative. Nevertheless, what can be said with some confidence is that whatever mistakes the Fed

17. The data were available (from the 1980 appendix to the annual Council of Economic Advisers report) only from 1960 onward, and annual estimates for all three variables were constructed by averaging year-end figures. The relationship was fit between total commercial bank deposits and member bank reserves.

has made, its management of money during the past three decades has given the economy a much more stable money supply.

Other Stabilizing Features of the Postwar Economy

Three features stand out when the behavior of the various components of GNP in the prewar period is compared with their behavior in the postwar period. First, the Keynesian multiplier was smaller—that is, fluctuations in nonconsumption elements of GNP induced larger fluctuations in consumption in the prewar period than in the postwar period. Second, the average ratio of gross private domestic investment to GNP was smaller in the postwar period. Third, the percentage fluctuations in investment were smaller.

Let us start with the behavior of consumption. Whereas the standard deviation of annual changes in GNP during the postwar period was 43 percent as large as in the prewar years, the standard deviation of changes in consumption was only 35 percent of its prewar value. A regression of annual changes in consumption on contemporaneous changes in the sum of all other components of GNP produces a prewar coefficient that is smaller than its postwar counterpart. The regression implies a crude Keynesian multiplier that was about 20 percent smaller in the postwar years than it had been earlier. Delong and Summers suggest two reasons why postwar consumption varied less relative to changes in GNP than did prewar consumption.[18] First, consumers possessed modest liquid assets, had little access to credit, and were much more constrained by their liquidity in the prewar period than in the postwar years. The large expansion in the availability of consumer credit has greatly improved the ability of households to smooth consumption during periods of income decline. Delong and Summers test this theory by an equation in which consumption is regressed on prior consumption and a current disposable income variable, itself estimated from a second-order autoregressive process. For the prewar years 1899–1916 they find consumption to be almost totally dependent on disposable income; the coefficient on prior

18. Delong and Summers, "Changing Cyclical Variability," pp. 24–31.

consumption was effectively zero. Consumers were highly constrained by lack of liquidity. In the postwar period Delong and Summers' estimates suggest that some, but not all, consumers were liquidity constrained. Little confidence, however, can be put on the magnitude of the postwar coefficients and thus on the relative weights to be given liquidity constraints versus consumption smoothing. Blinder and Deaton, in a recent analysis of postwar time series, conclude that both elements are important in the postwar years.[19]

Granted that liquidity constraints, though of reduced importance, have not been eliminated in the postwar period, the automatic stabilizing features of the postwar federal tax and transfer systems helped smooth disposable income and therefore consumption. Delong and Summers constructed an annual time series for prewar disposable income and found that the coefficient relating contemporaneous changes in disposable income to GNP during the postwar period is only about half the size of the corresponding coefficient for the 1899–1916 years.

Both a reduction in liquidity constraints and the smoothing of disposable income thus seem to have contributed to the greater stability of consumption in recent years, which can be summarized as a 20 percent decline in the value of the crude Keynesian multiplier between the prewar and postwar periods.

The second and third reasons for greater stability involve the behavior of investment. In both prewar and postwar periods private investment was the most volatile component of aggregate spending. The share of gross private domestic investment in total GNP fell from 0.20 in the early years to 0.15 in the postwar period, a decline of one-fourth. Its volatility, as measured by the standard deviation of annual percent changes, was 36 percent lower in the later period. Government purchases of goods and services were a small and relatively stable component of GNP in the prewar period. In the postwar years the government's share was, of course, much larger, and it was fairly stable from year to year. But interestingly, on average, government purchases of goods and services provided no countercyclical offset to

19. Alan S. Blinder and Angus Deaton, "The Time Series Consumption Function Revisited," BPEA, 2:1985, pp. 465–511.

changes in investment purchases. That is, when annual changes in both investment and government spending are measured as a percent of the previous year's GNP, the standard deviation of the sum of changes in investment and government purchases, so measured, is exactly the same as the standard deviation of investment changes alone.[20]

Let me try to put some of these comparisons in perspective. I assume the simplest Keynesian income determination process in which the annual percent change in GNP attributable to changes in investment is equal to the product of three numbers: the percent change in investment, the ratio of investment to GNP, and the multiplier. If, as stylized facts, one assumes that within each of the two periods there was no trend either in the ratio of gross private domestic investment to GNP or in the multiplier, then in each period the standard deviation of the annual percent change in GNP is approximately equal to the standard deviation of the percent change in investment multiplied by two constants—the multiplier and the ratio of investment to GNP. The ratio of the postwar to the prewar standard deviation of changes in GNP attributable to investment fluctuations will then be approximately equal to the product of three ratios: the ratio of the postwar to the prewar multiplier (0.82); the ratio of the postwar to the prewar investment share (0.76); and the ratio of the postwar to the prewar investment volatility measured by the standard deviation of annual percentage changes in investment (0.64). The product of these ratios is 0.40. The actual ratio of the postwar to the prewar standard deviation of changes in GNP is similar, 0.43.[21]

On this crude measure, the combination of greater consumption smoothing and a smaller share of investment in GNP would alone have dropped the postwar standard deviation of annual GNP changes to about 65 percent of its prewar level. For whatever combination of endogenous and exogenous factors, the decline in the volatility of

---

20. Let Y, G, and I be GNP, government purchases, and investment, respectively. Then, for the period 1953–83

$$\sigma\left[\frac{\Delta\,(G + I)}{Y_{-1}}\right] \cong \sigma\left[\frac{\Delta\,I}{Y_{-1}}\right].$$

21. See appendix C.

private investment accounted for much of the remaining decline in the standard deviation of GNP changes to 40 percent of the prewar level. If I am right about the nature of the change in the money supply function, part of the reason for the declining volatility of investment was the greater procyclical variation in interest rates resulting from the elimination of the earlier procyclical endogeneity of the money supply.

In a 1978 paper Baily offered a powerful additional reason for the reduced volatility of investment, one indirectly supported in a 1983 paper by Neary and Stiglitz.[22] Baily showed that if wages and prices are not completely flexible, anticipated policy that reduces the effect on output of demand shocks will cause investors to behave in a stabilizing way—that is, to respond to such shocks with smaller changes in investment. Neary and Stiglitz similarly argue that with sticky wages and prices, anticipated changes in policy are more rather than less effective in influencing output. More generally, nothing succeeds like success. Insofar as the managed money of the postwar period eliminated the procyclical shifts of the LM curve that had earlier afflicted the economy, gradual recognition of the consequences of this fact may itself have helped reduce the fluctuations in GNP. Stabilization of the LM curve eventually helped stabilize the IS curve.

Effects of Regressive Expectations during the Prewar Period

There is some evidence that expectations in the prewar economy were regressive about interest rates and that this expectational pattern may have had destabilizing effects on output. Long-term nominal interest rates in the prewar years showed little variance. As reported earlier, the standard deviation of annual changes in railroad bond yields was only twenty-four basis points. In those years there was no positive association between short- and long-term nominal interest rates and either current inflation or the one-year-ahead inflation

---

22. Martin Neil Baily, "Stabilization Policy and Private Economic Behavior," *BPEA*, 1:1978, pp. 11–59; and J. Peter Neary and Joseph E. Stiglitz, "Toward a Reconstruction of Keynesian Economics: Expectations and Constrained Equilibria," *Quarterly Journal of Economics*, vol. 98 (1983, *Supplement*), pp. 199–228.

forecast (using the inflation equation from lecture 1).[23] In the postwar period, however, there was a significant positive association between inflation and both the short- and long-term bond rate; a 1 percentage point change in the one-year-ahead inflation forecast, for example, was associated with a 0.8 to 0.9 percentage point change in short- and long-term nominal interest rates. The postwar relationship does not, of course, imply causality. But it does suggest that the factors generating cyclical changes in inflation also led to cyclical changes in interest rates in the postwar but not in the prewar period. Changes in long-term interest rates were also much less closely correlated with a three-year distributed lag of changes in short-term rates during the earlier period than in the postwar years. Both the sum of the coefficients and the $\bar{R}^2$ were much smaller in the prewar years.[24]

	1893–1914A	1893–1914B	1953–78
Sum of coefficients on short rate	0.39	0.28	0.84
	(2.6)	(2.5)	(9.7)
$\bar{R}^2$	0.32	0.30	0.79

Summers also found that during the early years (1860–1940 in his analysis) inflationary expectations had no significant effect on nominal interest rates.[25] He suggested that the lack of adjustment of nominal interest rates to inflation arose from money illusion. I also believe there was a failure to distinguish between real and nominal interest rates. This phenomenon, as well as the comparatively loose association between long-term bond yields and a distributed lag of short-term rates, may have arisen from the way in which the cyclical characteristics of the period affected the behavior of economic agents. The repeated, very rapid, and erratic cyclical swings in output created great uncer-

23. There was a small *negative* association between forecast inflation and the nominal bond rate.

24. The short rate was entered as an unconstrained first-order Almon lag covering the current and the two prior years. The A version incorporates the Federal Reserve-Mitchell series on short-term commercial paper rates; the B series employs the Macaulay estimates. See note 9. The numbers in parentheses are *t*-statistics.

25. Lawrence H. Summers, "The Non-Adjustment of Nominal Interest Rates: A Study of the Fisher Effect," National Bureau of Economic Research Working Paper 836 (Cambridge, Mass.: NBER, January 1982).

tainty in the very short run, and together with the lack of any persistence effect in inflation induced economic agents not to extrapolate current changes into the future. The best bet was to ignore short-run changes in prices and to expect them to regress toward their long-run trend value. Variations in short-term interest rates were relatively small to begin with, and those changes were less likely to persist for any length of time. To the extent that long-term rates bear some relationship to the average of expected short-term rates, there was thus very little room for long-term rates to move in a way that would help offset the swings in the schedule of the marginal efficiency of capital.

It might be argued that regressive inflation expectations should have helped to stabilize output. A decline in output and a fall in inflation, to the point where prices were lower than their trend path, would generate expectations of a subsequent increase in the inflation rate, and with relatively constant nominal interest rates these expectations would raise the demand for durable goods. This hypothesis implies that without regressive price expectations the prewar volatility of output would have been even larger than it actually was. A more likely interpretation of these facts is the one suggested above—the relative stability of nominal interest rates in the face of large swings in actual inflation is evidence that economic agents tended to ignore the difference between nominal and real interest rates. For that reason the relative lack of procyclical flexibility in short-term (nominal) interest rates and the small response of long-term rates to cyclical changes in short-term rates contributed to the volatility of output in the prewar economy.

Conclusion

I do not pretend that this review of comparative cyclical data has provided a comprehensive search for all the possible causes of the change in the U.S. economy's stability. But the review has suggested several propositions.

First, despite the supposed rigidity of the gold standard, the prewar monetary system was more accommodative to demand shocks than the managed money of the last four decades. The less accommodative postwar monetary system increased the procyclical characteristics of interest rates and helped stabilize the economy. Though mistakes were made in both directions, the overall effect on output stability of the Federal Reserve's money management has been beneficial.

Second, the path of consumption has been smoother in the postwar period, and that has contributed to the stability of output. Two causes for the greater smoothness of consumption can reasonably be extracted from the data: liquidity constraints on consumers have been reduced, and the effect of the remaining constraints have been moderated by the automatic stabilizing effects of the federal budget on disposable personal income.

Third, it is reasonable to hypothesize that success in reducing or eliminating the procyclical instability of the LM curve contributed toward the observed reduction in the instability of private investment.

Fourth, there is some (but not conclusive) evidence that in the prewar years inflation expectations were regressive on the price level. I think it possible that the nature of expectations about inflation (as well as about economic events generally) in the prewar period generated a stability in nominal long-run interest rates to the point that they did not very well serve the macroeconomic function of coordinating intertemporal choices among savers and investors. Potential saving-investment imbalances had to work themselves out principally through changes in income.

Appendix A:
A Demand-for-Money Function

Let

    MR = stock of real money balances, M2 (Friedman-Schwartz version)

    MR^* = desired stock of real money balances

    Q^N = potential GNP

    $\hat{Q}$ = ratio of actual to potential GNP

    R = commercial paper rate

    t = time

    D_{75} = dummy variable, taking on a value of 1.0 in 1975 and later years and 0 otherwise

    V_0 = base period velocity of real M2 (against potential GNP).

When lower case letters are used, they are natural logarithms, except for t.

The basic equation for money demand is given by

$$(A\text{-}1) \qquad MR^* = \left[\frac{Q^N}{V_0 e^{gt}} \right] \hat{Q}^\beta \, R^{-\theta} \, \delta_{75}.$$

Actual balances are assumed to adjust to desired balances according to

$$(A\text{-}2) \qquad \Delta\, mr = \lambda(mr^* - mr_{-1}).$$

The basic equation allows for a distinction between the effect of long-term increases in real income on the demand for money balances, given by the term $Q^N/V_0 e^{\lambda t}$, and the effect of cyclical changes in income given by $\hat{Q}$. As in all such equations, it is assumed that in the long run prices adjust so as to keep the demand and supply of real money balances equal, while in the short run interest rates and income do the adjusting.

Table A-1. *Demand for Money Regression Results*[a]

Independent variable	Prewar[b]		Postwar
	A	B	
Constant	−0.08	−0.14	−0.19
$(q^N - mr_{-1})$	0.340	0.294	0.320
	(2.7)	(2.3)	(5.5)
t	0.004	0.005	0.004
	(1.7)	(2.3)	(4.8)
r	−0.170	−0.120	−0.085
	(−3.5)	(−3.9)	(−8.9)
$\hat{q}$	0.558	0.613	0.631
	(4.1)	(4.8)	(7.1)
D_{75}	...	...	0.032
	...	...	(4.1)
Summary statistic			
$\bar{R}^2$	0.62	0.65	0.86
Durbin-Watson	1.80	1.86	2.05

Source: Author's calculations.

a. See the appendix text for the definition of the variables. The numbers in parentheses are t-statistics.

b. A version uses the Federal Reserve-Mitchell commercial paper rate; B version uses the Macaulay series. See note 9 in the text.

Converting to logs and substituting A-1 into A-2, one can fit the following equation:

$$\Delta mr_t = a_0 + a_1(q_t^N - mr_{-1})_t + a_2t + a_3\hat{q}_t - a_4r_t + a_5D_{75} + \epsilon_t,$$

where

$$-a_0 = v_0$$
$$a_1 = \lambda$$
$$-a_2/a_1 = g$$
$$a_3/a_1 = \beta$$
$$a_4/a_1 = \theta.$$

The results of fitting the equation to 1891–1914 and 1953–78 are shown in table A-1.

The implicit elasticities of the LM curves, $-(a_4/a_3)$, are

$$\text{Prewar A} = 0.31$$
$$\text{Prewar B} = 0.20$$
$$\text{Postwar} = 0.13.$$

If the supply of money is endogenous, then the underlying demand for money function cannot be identified. If the prewar money supply itself was a positive function of $\hat{Q}$ or r, this would produce the higher interest elasticity shown above, even if the interest elasticity of the demand for money function itself were no higher in the prewar than the postwar period.

Appendix B:
Relationships among Changes in Bank Deposits, Currency, Money Supply, and Bank Reserves

Let

$DM2$ = absolute change in M2

DCU = absolute change in currency

DBD = absolute change in bank deposits

$x = COVAR\ (DCU,\ DM2)/VAR\ (DM2)$ = simple regression coefficient of DCU on $DM2$

$y = COVAR\ (DBD,\ DM2)/VAR\ (DM2)$ = simple regression coefficient of DBD on $DM2$.

Since $DM2 = DCU + DBD$, then $x + y = 1.0$. In the period 1891–1914, $x = 0.04$ and $y = 0.96$. Thus during that period changes in M2 were typically composed of 96 percent of changes in bank deposits and 4 percent of changes in currency.

In a similar vein, after the data are converted to logs, the change in bank deposits is equal to the change in bank reserves plus the change in the deposit-to-reserve ratio. When the same techniques as set forth above are used, the results are as given in the text: only 43 percent of the annual variance of changes in bank deposits was associated with changes in bank reserves, and all the rest came from changes in the ratio of deposits to reserves. In the postwar years 1961–79, 91 percent of the annual variance in bank deposits was associated with the variance in reserves.

Appendix C:
Contribution of Lower Investment Volatility and Greater Consumption Stability to the Reduction of Output Fluctuations, Postwar versus Prewar Years

Let

$\bar{s}_{1,2}$ = the average share of investment in GNP in the early and postwar years

$\bar{m}_{1,2}$ = the multiplier in each of the two periods, assumed to be constant throughout the period

$\sigma(q)_{1,2}$ = the standard deviation of the annual percent change in GNP attributable to investment fluctuations

$\sigma(v)_{1,2}$ = the standard deviation of the annual percent change in investment (the base on which the percent change is measured in any year is $\bar{s}q_t$).

Then
$$(\bar{s})(\bar{m})(v_t) \cong q_t,$$

and since the standard deviation of the product of a constant and a variable is the constant times the standard deviation of the variable, then

$$\sigma(q) \cong \bar{s} \, \bar{m} \, \sigma(v)$$

and
$$\frac{\sigma(q)_2}{\sigma(q)_1} \cong \frac{\bar{s}_2}{\bar{s}_1} \times \frac{\bar{m}_2}{\bar{m}_1} \times \left[\frac{\sigma(v)_2}{\sigma(v)_1} \right].$$

Index